Given by Esther Browning
died March 1993.

LLOYD GEORGE

Lloyd George.

LLOYD GEORGE

by

EARL LLOYD GEORGE

FREDERICK MULLER LIMITED
LONDON

FIRST PUBLISHED IN 1960 IN GREAT BRITAIN BY
FREDERICK MULLER LIMITED
PRINTED AND BOUND BY
HAZELL WATSON AND VINEY LTD
AYLESBURY AND SLOUGH

CONTENTS

ILLUSTRATIONS

Retrospect

MY mother was one of those rare, inwardly serene persons who believe that death is a beginning; and in the winter of 1941, when she died, some of this tranquillity was communicated to me and I had no sense of final loss or even grief.

I went down calmly to the kitchen and enquired whether there would be enough food for the people who attended the funeral. Those were days of austerity and rationing, but the refrigerator was stocked with chickens, hams enough to feed a battalion. From miles around neighbours had anticipated this problem for us.

I tried to keep myself busy with preparations for the funeral. I was worried about my father, then in his seventy-eighth year. He had tried to reach mother at her bedside during her fatal illness, and thinking it would be quicker to go by road, he was caught in blizzards of snow that buried the car in snowdrifts repeatedly. (Half the countryside turned out to help dig him out and speed him on his journey.) When he arrived at Criccieth it was too late. He broke down, and I was deeply concerned that the shock of mother's death, his failure to reach her in time, would prostrate him.

He looked dreadful, poor old fellow, grey and frail and pathetic; and coming off the train, he threw his arms round me and wept.

I think that was the moment when my mind cleared about him, when the bitter conflict of feeling I had known towards him most of the years of my life was resolved, and I had a sense of objectivity, even of protectiveness towards him. I knew that it was as much a sense of guilt towards my mother as sorrow for her that wrung his heart; and that he should have turned to me at that moment after so many years of coldness between us was a plea, if not for forgiveness—he was always too arrogant for that—then for a judgment in human terms, in worldly terms. I was his eldest child, his first-born; and I had demanded much from him as my right. All the adult years I had endeavoured to be my mother's

9

shield. I had been an angry son to my father. I had tried always not to be self-righteous.

Thus will I try to judge my father, in human terms, in worldly terms, if I am able to, with dispassion, but always with compassion because even my deepest anger had been edged with love.

The evening before the funeral was fine and radiant—a bad sign, because in Snowdonia this is almost certainly an indication of bad weather for the morrow; but strangely and hearteningly the next day was clear and brilliant with sun on the mountains and the valley—as though my mother had smiled on this day, it seemed to my foolish filial heart; and as our many friends drew the wagon along the steep and slippery slope, glittering with sun on snow, to the family vault where my sister lay, I thought with deeper sadness of father than mother. For him death was a perplexing mystery.

'Once, when she was planting seedlings,' I said to him, 'she spoke of death as the only verity. Birth can be misconceived, and in any case one begins the process of dying the moment one is born. It is the only "truth", and she always accepted it.'

I thought, as I looked at him, it was only a sorrow for the living. How would he approach it at the end? With what thoughts and feelings? He would die as he had always lived, a pagan. He was a great Bible-quoter, father. He knew all the words. He was the greatest Bible-thumping pagan of his generation.

He gave me one of his quizzical glances from under those bushy eyebrows, and then a tender look; and my feelings went out to him.

We laid my mother to rest beside my sister's grave, his best-beloved child, who had died when she was only seventeen. It had been my father's most enduring sorrow.

I thought of my father.

I shall try to put down in this book some of these thoughts. I am seventy, and my memory reaches back to many incidents. In parts it is good and my recollection clear; at other times it is hazy and I can only recall general impressions and feelings. Then, my facts may be wrong; places and dates are confused. This is not a faithful and accurate portrayal of historic facts, but for these the reader can consult official texts. I have tried to concern myself with truth, with the essence of things, and with those strange, wayward and subtle meanings behind facts. It is a broken lamp, my memory, faulty and inefficient, but it may throw a little light on the enigma of a man who has been described as the greatest Prime Minister since Pitt.

WELSH CLANSMAN

1

LORD BOOTHBY has described Lloyd George as one of two authentic political geniuses in British politics this century, the other being Winston Churchill, and this reminds me of the youthful question I asked my father many years ago: 'When did you first suspect you were a genius?'

It was not intended ironically (not altogether); and my father tapped me solemnly on the shoulder and said, 'Suspect? Suspect? I *knew*. It does not follow that everyone who believes himself to be one is a genius, of course; but no genius fails to know he is one.'

'When did you first believe yourself to be one?' I asked him.

'Early. Very early,' my father said. 'As a matter of fact, I was a boy at the time. I liked to climb a certain oak tree and sit perched up high in the branches. Now this was not the hallmark of genius, of course. Most boys in the district liked climbing trees. But I was the only one who, when he got up to sit on the top branch, took out a copy of *Euclid* and began to study it. On one occasion when I did this the singular thought struck me, "What a remarkable fellow am I, to read *Euclid* on top of an oak tree. Why am I doing this?" I asked myself. And, quick as a flash, I answered myself, "I am special. I am astonishing. *Duw*, I believe I am a genius."'

'What made you sit on top of an oak tree to read *Euclid*?'

'The Olympian heights. The detachment that comes from a proper understanding of the spirit of mathematics,' my father said, or words to that effect; and then he wandered off into the world of his private thoughts.

Such tantalising fragments of conversation stick in the memory.

My father fascinated me. As a boy, he was a profound mystery to me. In the naïve, candid manner of childhood, I asked him endless questions which sometimes he showed a remarkable patience in answering, but more often he dismissed them because his head was busy with Olympian and detached thoughts about lofty subjects; he often sat on top of his oak tree even in the midst of his family circle.

As a boy, a country boy brought up in Caernarvon, he was not always remarkable, although he was almost always a leader. The man my father became—solicitor, statesman, orator, author, newspaper proprietor—never lost the boy. His roots remained in the soil. He loved farming. He preferred the country to the city. Many years later, when he was being shown the industrial marvels of the Third Reich, he wearied quickly and cut short his tour of the factories; but he showed endless interest in the vast new agricultural projects. He pulled up and examined the roots of a potato plant and, nodding sagely, astonished his companions by saying, 'This is an excellent crop. It will yield ten to twelve tons an acre.' (He was right.)

He loved the earth; he loved his native country ways; he was a master of his native language. He was proud of all these qualities.

It was not difficult to understand his pleasure in these things. North Wales, in spite of some beastly weather—it has about the highest rainfall in the United Kingdom—is one of the most beautiful places on earth, and whenever he was exhausted with the hurly-burly of high politics, he would take a trip home. The first sight of the Welsh hills would instantly revive his spirits, rejuvenate him and endue him with fresh energy. It had the same effect on my mother.

His boyhood home was set in the midst of woodland, valley, sparkling water; and the light on the hills changed from apple-green in the morning to misty purple at night. The countryside teemed with small game; the streams shimmered with trout; and, in spite of the ominous presence of the gamekeeper, there was sport in abundance to supplement the delectable menu of home-cooked dishes—Welsh dishes such as home-baked oatcakes and pancakes and bread of a score of varieties.

The orchards were raided, too, and as a boy he not only joined such expeditions, he was almost invariably the 'brains' of the gang. He became a great fruit grower in later life, with such excellent results that windfalls were often sold to Fortnum's at top prices; and I would often divert a manifestation of bad temper by a hasty reference to the wonderful progress the rhubarb was making.

Everybody who remembers him, thinks of my father as a fiery Welshman; and, in fact, he never did become Anglicised. He never allowed you to forget what he was and where he came from. His speeches, which sometimes slipped into Welsh when he got carried away, were freely embellished with analogies about valleys and mountain summits, or woods and storms, all the elemental images which featured in the framework of his native country.

Here is an extract from a speech he made when he was Chancellor of the Exchequer:

'Yesterday I visited the old village where I was brought up. I wandered through the woods familiar to my boyhood. There I saw a child gathering sticks for firewood, and I thought of the hours I spent in the same pleasant and profitable occupation, for I also have been something of a backwoodsman. And here is one experience taught me then which is of use to me today. I learned as a child it was little use going into the woods after a period of calm and fine weather, for I generally returned almost empty-handed. But after a great storm, I came back with an armful. We are in for rough weather now; we may even be in for a winter of storms which will rock the forest, break many a withered branch, and leave many a rotten tree torn up by the roots. But when the weather clears, you may depend on it there will be something brought within the reach of the people that will give warmth and glow to their grey lives, something that will help to dispel the hunger, the despair, the oppressions and the wrong which now chill so many of their hearths.'

These brilliant, eloquent images, which seemed to spring spontaneously from the roots of the man, echoing his childhood upbringing, stamped him as a great Welsh patriot, the personality of popular conception.

David Lloyd George, in fact, was born in Manchester in 1863. I once asked him, whilst he was expounding some point of Welsh nationalism with eloquence, 'You're a Mancunian by birth. Don't you ever identify yourself with Manchester and the English?'

He laughed. 'National feeling has nothing to do with geography, Dick. It's a state of mind. Empire Day is celebrated much more fervently in some African village than in London. Napoleon, who spread the French flag over most of Europe, was a Corsican. De Valera, democratically appointed leader of Irish nationalists, is an American of semi-Spanish extraction.'

My father's nationalism was, in fact, a 'state of mind'. Although born on English soil, and although he lived most of his life in England, he always identified himself with the country where he spent his boyhood and youth. The Welsh think of themselves as a race of poets and warriors; and, as a minority race, they have been forced often to adopt the rôle of rebels. These are the characteristics which appealed to my father. In the same way that he dramatised his appearance by wearing his hair long and donning a Tyrolean cloak, so he adopted mentally the dramatic traits that provided him with so much ammunition as a politician. Knowing my father as I did, I am not altogether sure that this was not a deliberate theatrical device because, although he was often a rebel, he was never a revolutionary, and his many protestations of Welsh nationalism never took the form of advocating fully independent status for Wales.

On the other hand, I am sure that much of his feeling for the Welsh was absolutely genuine. He spent his childhood in the little villages that cling to the blue hills of Caernarvon, and it was there, after the long turbulent odyssey of his career, that he retired to spend the twilight of his life.

My father's antecedents were farmers, and he claimed that his great-grandmother caused the rout of some French soldiers, a revolutionary contingent that had landed near Fishguard. Great-grandmother dressed a party of housewives in scarlet cloaks and paraded them on the heights above the French troops. The women were mistaken for British Redcoats, and the French surrendered without a fight. This camouflage technique greatly appealed to my father, and he was fond of relating this story to indicate the early manifestation of Lloyd Georgian tactical skill.

Lloyd George's father was a schoolmaster, a sensitive, gentle person, who suffered from serious ill health. He had to give up his work in Manchester and return to his native Wales, as it was considered that an outdoor farming life might restore his strength. Unfortunately, he caught a chill, developed pneumonia, and died shortly after, leaving a widow and two small children.

The bereaved family were fortunate in possessing a relative of remarkable character, 'Uncle Lloyd', who came promptly to their aid. Richard Lloyd was my grandmother's brother, who took on the responsibility of providing for the fatherless family. In answer to a two-word telegram—'Come, Richard'—he immediately set out to comfort his sister, In a twenty-mile spell, he walked the distance from Criccieth to the railway station near Caernarvon, and there took the train to Bwlford in South Wales, where his sister awaited him.

He took the family home with him to Llanystumdwy, where they lived together in a five-room cottage. Richard Lloyd was a shoe-maker, with a workshop next door, who earned a living sufficient to care for and feed the new additions to his homestead; but it was not enough to support a marriage, too, so Richard Lloyd denied himself the comfort of a wife. His sister and her children became his whole family, and their upbringing became the main purpose of his existence.

He was a fine-looking man, tall, bearded, with the face of an apostle. He was the only man I knew who could dominate my father, and this he did by personality and moral force entirely; for although these were mid-Victorian days he never raised a hand to his adopted sons.

A deep affection and life-long friendship and respect rewarded his devotion. My father, who was the world's worst correspondent during the busiest period of his political life, never failed to write to him; and he drew strength and courage from the letters he regularly received from a village shoe-maker in North Wales.

It was a good life for the children, a healthy country existence; and in addition, there was a devotion to their mental life of a very high order, for Richard Lloyd was a life-long student of philosophy and theology, a lay preacher, with the greatest respect and admiration for learning and moral precept. He was a Baptist and a Radical Liberal.

There is no doubt that David Lloyd George's young mind was the driest of tinder to the intellectual fire which assailed it; and although he did not long accept the 'catastrophist' beliefs of the strict interpretation of the Scriptures favoured by his uncle, there is nothing like a good theological argument to sharpen the polemical faculty, and he learned very early all the debating principles of importance, including the necessity to have a thorough grounding in his subject. He steeped himself in Bible-reading not because he had any special regard for religion, but in order to cap quotations with more trenchant references of his own.

Besides, the chapel, with its unpaid preacher, was the combination tribune and theatre where the verities were most dramatically expounded, and emotion coloured all expressions of faith. To Lloyd George an argument without emotion and drama was like bread without salt.

Another important village forum was the blacksmith's shop, where every conceivable subject, religious or secular, was thoroughly debated. There was one poor fellow who had started as a quarryman, but when the depression in the slate pits caused him to be laid off, he emigrated to the coalfields in South Wales. He worked there for a time, and then had the misfortune to lose a leg in an accident. He returned to his old home in Llanystumdwy, and pottered about on his peg until his death. After the funeral, a discussion and debate arose in the smithy. On the Great Day—the Day of Resurrection—would Poor Tom have to trail down to South Wales to look for his leg, or would it be miraculously conveyed and re-joined to the bereaved body? Such were the splendid human topics that had to be fitted into universal laws of gospel; and many years later, when the streets of the great cities as well as the small villages had their Poor Toms hobbling on wooden pegs, I remember my father recalling all the arguments of the smithy debate and drawing reassurance from nostalgic recollections.

My father's religious beliefs fluctuated; and there were periods in his life when he lost faith. He once asked me if I believed in prayer. I was a youngster in those days, and I made some undergraduate retort to the effect that when I was in a jam I would pray in the fervent hope of getting some sort of miraculous aid to my problem. He said to me, 'There have been times when I prayed—prayed desperately; but there seemed to be no one at the other end of the telephone.'

This scepticism manifested itself very early indeed, in spite of the preponderant religious influence in his boyhood. He told me of an occasion when he felt so conscience-stricken about his doubts that he even bearded the prophet himself, Uncle Lloyd; and to his astonishment and relief the anticipated typhoon of remonstrance did not blow. There was only a moment of deep quiet, a look of grave concern, and the gentle zephyr: 'Faith is a candle flame that often flickers. You have to guard it at all times.'

'And if it becomes extinguished?'

'It is always possible to relight the candle,' Uncle Lloyd said.

Living with Uncle Lloyd, it was easy to have faith; his God was such a tolerant and human manifestation.

My father found it difficult to accept the Baptist creed—the sect was known as the Disciples of Christ—in one of its cardinal tenets, that of the literal interpretation of the Bible; but this did not prevent him from organising a schoolboy rebellion against the Church of England teachings. The fact was that in those days the schools were owned by the English Church, and the Nonconformist faiths were not taught there; but the Church of England doctrines were liberally expounded, and thus it became a principle of national and family loyalty to oppose them.

One day, in anticipation of a school visit by two important personages, the Squire and the Rector, Master David called a meeting of the pupils and exhorted them to a certain conspiracy of protest, known technically in the army as mute insubordination.

It was an early essay in advocacy, and succeeded in whipping up such support that the next day, when the headmaster began to demonstrate to the distinguished visitors his pupils' thorough religious indoctrination, he was suddenly confronted by a complete blankness, a total eclipse of memory on a communal scale. The distinguished visitors looked astonished; the headmaster turned pale, then pink. He repeated the first question of the Catechism, and instead of the unfailing dirge-like response, an owlish stare of incomprehension greeted him. He tried desperately yet again; the entire school of pupils sat in coma, miraculously smitten with a simultaneous amnesia.

'What is thy duty to thy neighbour?'

No one seemed to have the faintest inkling.

'I believe——' urged the headmaster.

'I believe——' he repeated.

The pupils seemed to wait with baited breath for his pro-
nouncement of faith.

But when he repeated it once more, and in a very ominous
tone, a treble voice tremulously responded. It was Master David's
younger brother, William, whose nerve had failed him. Perhaps,
he thought that the ringleader would suffer some dreadful penalty
if the revolt continued.

It was the first breach in the defence. One by one the other
pupils responded, until schoolboy voices were raised in monoton-
ous unison, responding in the orthodox fashion.

The rebellion was at an end.

Master David did not forgive the traitor. After school, he set
upon him with his fists and gave him a good hiding.

Apart from national and family loyalty, Lloyd George had
other objections to Church of England teachings. He despised
parrot-like incantations, mere conditioning of faith. Religion had
to be a potent, a living thing, humanly demonstrable; and if not
always explicable, its mystery had to excite the mind and the
emotions. He loved a good sermon, much in the way he enjoyed
a brilliant speech or a fine piece of choral singing; and whether he
believed or not, the theatre appealed to him, and the poetry, and
the crusading spirit—the contest of faiths that involved Us and
Them.

In later years, he would tell 'preaching' stories in a way I have
never known equalled, and in a way which later generations would
probably find unique. He would tell them with the uninhibited
pleasure with which other men would relate anecdotes of politics
or gallantry.

Here are two of the stories:

The Reverend Herbert Evans was answering critics of the
Bible: 'I recently visited a little chapel in the Pennant Valley.
When the service was concluded an old lady came to me and said,
"Mr Evans, you will be staying overnight with us. But it is very
dark and stormy tonight, the path is very treacherous and long,
and full of pitfalls. Here is a little lamp. It is old and full of holes;
and there are rents in it; but it will give you enough light to see
you safely home." The five Books of Moses may be full of holes
and imperfections. They are wrong about places and dates, and

you can pick rents in them, pick them to pieces. But they shed enough light to show you the true path.'

And this, which was always my father's favourite:

Jesus was sleeping in the boat bound for Bethsaida. A great storm gradually arose, but he remained sleeping. John and Peter conferred in the boat as to what should be done. 'It is dangerous. We cannot go on. Let us turn back,' said John. 'No,' said Peter, 'the Master said we must go to Bethsaida.' John consulted with James and together they went to Peter. 'James agrees. It is too dangerous to go on. We must return,' said John.—'No,' said Peter.—'But if we sink?' protested James.—'If we sink,' said Peter, 'the boat will go down with its bow pointing towards Bethsaida.'

2

DRAMATISED excerpts from the Bible were not, of course, the only mental influences on the young Lloyd George. He was a voracious reader of almost anything he could lay his hands on at the time, and this included many of the great classics, Dickens, Shakespeare and Defoe in particular. He read a great deal of history. The American Civil War profoundly interested him—Lincoln was his great idol. He steeped himself in the story of the French Revolution, and the personalities of the Tribune fascinated him. In later life, one of the most cherished possessions in his collection of curios and marvels was a document said to have been stained with the blood of Robespierre.

The blood of Robespierre may well have symbolised much of his youthful rebellious fervour, because those were days of brutal oppression for the Welsh. Whilst recently enfranchised by Gladstone's Bill, the tenant farmers were nevertheless to place their homes and livelihoods in jeopardy in voting against the Tory candidates. There was no secret ballot, and those who dared to vote Liberal were immediately victimised.

Many years later Lloyd George recalled his feelings far more eloquently than I can convey them in this narrative:

'I was a boy at school then, and I was in the blackest Tory parish in the land. I believe that my old uncle was the only Liberal in the village, though not the only Liberal in the parish. There were three or four in the parish besides him. One or two of them refused to vote for the Tory candidate, and two or three actually went further and dared to record their votes for the Liberal. All of them received notice to quit. I remember that some of the lads who were at school with me in the same class in a year or two had to leave the neighbourhood. I was very young, but lads do not forget things of that sort. I knew the reason why they left—because the great Squire of the Parish had turned their fathers out of their homes purely because they dared to vote for the Liberal candidate. The next quarter day, after the election, notices were showered upon the tenants. They were turned out by the score on to the roadside because they had dared to vote according to their consciences. But they woke the spirit of the mountains, that fought the might of the Normans for two centuries. There was such a feeling aroused among the people that, ere it was done, the political power of landlordism in Wales was shattered as effectively as the power of the Druids. It is my first memory of politics.'

After all these years, I can hear him say, 'the blackest Tory parish in the land' with that curious controlled emotion that was his when he really felt things very deeply; and his simple observation, 'It is my first memory of politics' struck me most vividly at the time. Lloyd George's simple utterances were always the truest and most eloquent. He was an influential man at the time when he spoke these words, and numbered many Tories amongst his friends—in fact, during his political life he only numbered Liberal leaders amongst his personal enemies—but this first experience of the workings of Tory landlordism was a crucial one which focused his political viewpoint forever.

Then there was the time the military were called out over the sore question of tithes. These were imposed on the tenant farmers for the upkeep of a church to which they did not subscribe— what could be a more infuriating imposition! The Nonconformists refused to pay them, and there was real trouble. The soldiers clashed with the tenant farmers in places like Blaenau Ffestiniog, the little town set at the foot of a sheer mountain that rises above it like a stone bastion—goats and sheep and hill ponies graze above the rooftops, and here there were ugly skirmishes and bloody heads. How thickly my father's brows gathered as he described the sinister background to the tragic scene. He would stamp about the room and brandish his fists as though calling down the mountain spirit to strike down the oppressors!

In his youth, Lloyd George had no fears of radicalism. He attended a meeting shunned by orthodox Liberals, held by a couple of genuine revolutionaries, Michael Davitt and Michael Jones, who advocated communal use of the land and all its fruits—

farming, gaming, fishing—a very daring policy in those days. He gave such a spirited vote of thanks to the two speakers that applause ran on for several minutes. After the meeting, he took Michael Davitt, who was a formidable and turbulent Irish Nationalist M.P. (unable to sit in Parliament at the time because he had recently been jailed for his Fenian activities) to a friend's home for supper.

'You should go into politics, my boy,' Davitt told him that evening. He had been impressed by his 'vote of thanks' speech at the meeting, and the long, searching discussion about the Rights of Man at supper brought the two of them close in sympathy.

I think it was the first contact Lloyd George had with politics in the raw as far as Socialist thinking was concerned, and undoubtedly he was somewhat attracted by them at the time; but the left-wingers of the Welsh race are a phenomenon of South Wales, not from the milder and more temperate farming community of the north. I know he always felt this difference. Had he been brought up in the mining districts of Wales, where the class struggle superseded the national fight for independence, he might well have swung to the extreme wing of politics, but he was essentially a traditionalist at the time—in the footsteps of reformers and not revolutionaries. Abraham Lincoln was a far more alluring model than Fouché.

We discussed this matter many years later, and it was always Honest Abe who was put forward as a sort of political father figure—a great crusader, a champion of the oppressed, but with his loyalties deeply involved with the tradition and culture of his country.

'You never know. Those Reds might even abolish performances of Shakespeare because he wrote the history of England through the stories of Kings and Queens!' he once said to me in a rather mock alarmist manner; and although it was part jest, there was an undercurrent that indicated fear of the break with tradition in any radical upheaval. On the other hand, he rather liked revolutionaries, whom he thought thundering good personalities. Anybody who could blaze a trail or make a loud individual noise—Lloyd George had a soft spot for him. I think that this was the reason why he later made so many excuses for Hitler, who greatly im-

26

pressed him when they met, and why he so much regretted Lenin's absence from the Genoa Conference. He got on excellently with the Irish nationalists, such as Michael Collins, who had a price on his head at the time of their meeting; and whenever there were serious labour problems, the government sent for Lloyd George to talk sweet reason to the agitators—which he did with the greatest effect.

He had so much imagination and ginger that he could forgive a politician almost any fault except insipidity.

As a boy he loved a good storm. The winter weather in the hills was wild, with sudden eruptions of thunder and lightning flash that often drew him out on lonely tramps even into dangerous places—woods and forests—or right up hill-tops, singing or declaiming passages from the classics. I remember one night at home—many years later, of course—when I was awakened by the noise of a thunderstorm. Being unable to sleep, I got out of bed and went for a walk through the house. I found my father sitting by the french windows of the library, with an open book on his knees.

'What are you reading?'

'Shakespeare.'

'Well, why not put the light on? You can't read in the dark.'

He made one of his sweeping gestures. 'Ever tried to read *King Lear* by flashes of lightning, Dick?'

I could see the eternal boy then, whose soul could tolerate anything except mediocrity, anything except the commonplace.

Very early in his life, he had this sort of passion for the written as well as the spoken word.

I once expressed to him an interest in a certain historical event. He promptly picked out a book for me, handling it with great care. He gave it to me, solemnly exhorting me to 'taste every word on the palate, like a good wine'. It was a bulky volume of Macaulay, and I regret to say that a fortnight later I had only tasted a very few of the vintage phrases. He buttonholed me some time later and demanded to know how I was getting on with the book. I confessed that I hadn't cut many pages. 'When I was a youngster,' he said to me with paternal melancholy, 'I walked seven miles to Portmadoc to get a newspaper in order to read a speech of Mr Gladstone's. And you have only to reach out a hand!'

I know it was no empty paternal boast; he took Uncle William with him on that route march.

My father took his exams to become a solicitor; and this was something of a marvel. The tiny village school was the only place of education he ever attended. Most readers will remember Emlyn Williams' warm and delightful *The Corn is Green*, the story of the ambitious schoolboy in the little Welsh village who was coached for an exam to Oxford by the devoted old school ma'am. It could have been patterned on my father's schooldays. To ensure attendance every week, each pupil had to fetch a penny on Monday and place it on the teacher's desk. The three R's were taught, and later history and some geography; and, if the pupil was exceptional, algebra. In order to take the first law exams, Latin and French had to be studied, and neither subject was taught at the school. My father was determined to be a lawyer. (He could not earn a living as a Baptist minister; and as sickness was about the only thing he feared in his life—that is, sickness and suffering in others—medicine was a closed door to him.) He would have greatly preferred to be a barrister, but there was not enough money to see him through the lean period in every barrister's early life, so it had to be as a solicitor that he would fashion a career.

How to overcome the problems of Latin and French? Here it was that Uncle Lloyd showed the mettle that put drive into his determination to succeed. He bought the necessary text-books, and at the age of fifty—without any former knowledge of a word of either language—he sat down to master them, battling every inch of the way to keep always one lesson ahead of his nimble-witted pupil. Every evening, after school, 'teacher' and pupil sat in the kitchen, and by the light of the paraffin lamp, pored over the conjugations of the irregular verbs and painfully and painstakingly followed the fortunes of the Gallic campaigns.

Lloyd George passed all his exams after years of such study. He was articled to a country firm, and in due course put up his sign D. Lloyd George, solicitor, in the shade of the walls of Criccieth Castle, which had never more proudly hoisted a banner.

He was a good solicitor, and the firm he founded became one of the most famous in Wales. He dealt patiently and industriously with the small problems posed by the tenant farmers, making a name for himself in the district county and police courts. He was careful and punctilious, learning the importance of being absolutely well-briefed for his appearances in court. Being a one-man concern, he had to be his own solicitor and advocate; there was no margin for error, so every detail, however trifling, had to be double-checked.

He later told me how important this was to him when he first entered Parliament. 'What most new members in the House fail to realise is the importance of parliamentary procedure—for instance, how to frame an amendment. They think it's all drama and fireworks. Eloquence isn't enough. You have to learn what the tools are made of before you learn how to use them.'

In the local courts the justices and magistrates gave a courteous hearing to the young advocate—he was twenty-one when he began his legal career. At first there were no 'fireworks' at all, and discussing this early period with him one day, I asked him why he had been relatively so restrained in the courts and so peppery in the debating clubs. 'I had a respect—a reverence, you might say—for institutions of authority. The political debates—that was something else. We were exchanging ideas. In the courts, a man's home or livelihood or liberty might be involved.'

But there were fireworks later, just the same; and at least one case that brought him national fame.

The restraint he showed in the courtroom certainly did not extend to his journalistic activities at the time. Under the *nom de guerre* 'Brutus', he wrote some very truculent pieces on political subjects which editors of local papers seemed pleased to publish. These efforts, unpaid but highly relished just the same, showed a youthful enthusiasm and a literary style characterised by all the deeper shades of the spectrum. Writing about the Tory colonial policy, this passage illustrates his more florid manner: 'Whose policy made Afghan mothers husbandless, their children fatherless and both homeless—saturated the Afghan snows with the blood of patriots, and drove hatred of our very name and presence into the heart of the Afghan nation? Whose policy made Zululand mourn the loss of its brave sons, devastated its fertile plains, turned its happy kraals into sombre mortuaries, and sacrificed its nationality upon a pyre erected with the carcases of its defenders?'

'I suppose you thought of yourself as the young Macaulay when you wrote this?' I asked him.

'I suppose I did.'

'Did you write it from the head or from the heart? I mean, what did you honestly care about the Zulus?'

'That's a question that should never be asked a politician.'

My father was often very quick with his answers to questions of this sort. He was not an impromptu orator in the manner, say, of F. E. Smith—he would take very great care in the preparation of speeches even in those days—and his seemingly spontaneous manner was due to a prodigious, well-trained memory; but he had a way with questioners and hecklers. My favourite story about those early days concerned a heckler who rudely interrupted at a meeting with a reference to his humble origin. 'What's happened to the cart and donkey?' he shouted, referring to the transport my grandmother used when she was collecting accounts for her brother, the shoe-maker. Lloyd George said, 'The cart—that's been chopped up for firewood long ago. But I'm happy to say the donkey is still with us. I heard him braying just a moment ago.' And the whimsical glance he gave the heckler set up a roar of laughter.

This, then, is a sketch of Lloyd George on his public occasions, the face he presented to the world in his boyhood and early manhood—dutiful and affectionate son and nephew, brilliant scholar, young professional man, debater and journalist; but one knows that he did not pass through the emotional phases of adolescence and vigorous, precocious youth without experiencing the sense of his growing life within him. Biographers seem to share the pretence that this emotional life was either non-existent or unimportant. In fact, it is quite impossible to understand the man and his character and career without a knowledge of his personal life.

As a child he had his fill of affection, which was a fine thing for him; it gave him a remarkable self-confidence most of the years of his life; it endowed him with a sense of compassion and of tolerance. But he was, in a sense, 'spoiled'—he himself admitted this; and this made him selfish, self-indulgent and unconsciously cruel—all his life he alternated cruelty with tender-heartedness, generosity with meanness. Almost the only true friend he was able to make in his life was Uncle Lloyd; and there were other remarkable and unexpected facets of his personality which appear to be entirely enigmatic until explained in psychological terms.

I know very little about the period of his adolescence and early manhood, but judging by the pattern of his life as I knew it later, he was undoubtedly up to all sorts of early essays and experiments in the arts of living and loving. It must be remembered that even in Victorian days fear and guilt about sex were mainly character-istic of urban and middle-class morality. Lloyd George had almost no inhibitions about these things—his religious beliefs were super-ficial, even though he could throw up a smoke screen of quota-tions from the scriptures, like a squid squirting ink, to conceal the paganism of his soul.

He was brought up as a country boy, and with his agile intelli-gence and insatiable mental curiosity, the facts of life could not have long remained a mystery to him. Every child brought up in a farming community soon learns from the mating habits of the beasts of the field the simple explanation to the secret stirrings within him.

It will be realised, too, that in those days and in that part of the country, there was almost no form of entertainment which did not involve personal relations. You could not slip quietly into a cinema to while away a few hours, or pay a visit to a restaurant or art gallery or theatre. Neither could you get the sort of distraction provided in these days by the mid-century gadgets, radios and television sets. Even the tavern or drinking-house was not what we know them to be these days. A great movement for temper-ance was sweeping over the country. Lloyd George never set foot inside a public-house during all this period of his life.

I remember a rather revealing conversation I once had with my father about romantic attachments. I was on holiday from Cam-bridge, and strongly attracted by a young lady whom I wanted to take out. Short of money as usual, I asked my father for a fiver, explaining why I needed it.

'What are you going to do? Where are you taking her?' he said in a friendly and humorous way.

'Oh, Scott's, I suppose. Lobster and a bottle. And then Daly's for a musical.'

'The art of courtship is a lost art,' he said, handing me the money. 'You take a girl to a restaurant where you don't have to open your mouth except to put food and drink in it. Nevertheless, the lady is soon mellowed and floating on air. Then you whisk her off in a cab to a place where all the serenading is done for you by a professional orchestra and three or four assorted groups of tenors and sopranos; and ballads composed by trained lyricists are sung in her ear, all by proxy. How would you fancy trying your hand with a girl when you've only got thruppence in your breeches and the only place you can take her is for a walk in the rain? (It was usually raining.)' My father added this final parenthetical comment with one of his knowing grins.

'And how did you get on?' I challenged.

'We got wet.'

He regarded me with a paternal cynicism, as though wondering what stuff *I* was made of; and he had no need to enlarge on his final remark.

I have an old photograph before me, as I write these words of my father, when he was a youth of seventeen. He wore his hair shorter in those days, and his clear, youthful features are much finer than in photographs of him as a man, the brows high, the expression serious and even intense. It is a remarkably handsome face, almost satanically handsome in a Byronic way. And how impeccable his sartorial style—the snug cravat, the romantic high collar, the smoothly-draped jacket. For a poor country youth, his care for and sense of his personal appearance were extraordinary.

Lloyd George always knew exactly what he wanted; and he came to terms early with himself.

My parents with Mair Eiluned (who died in 1907) and Megan.

Gwilym, Mair, myself and Olwen with my mother and (in front) Megan.

3

MY father's meeting with my mother was not a case of love at first sight, although she was greatly stimulated by his personality and impressed by his mental force. How and where they met it is difficult to ascertain now, but when speaking of it mother made it clear that at the time both of them regarded the occasion as an important one.

My mother, Maggie Owen then, was a warm, vivacious and quick-witted girl who was regarded as one of the belles of the county. Her affectionate upbringing—she was an only child—gave her a certain stability and poise. I think it was the sense of her inner calm that particularly drew the turbulent-natured David Lloyd George, who needed above all things anchorage for a rebellious and restless spirit. I think it could not have taken my father long to recognise Maggie Owen's qualities—complete honesty in personal relationships, loyalty and a capacity for protective womanly love.

This is not speculation: in the many years of their marriage it was always my mother who through the great-hearted tolerance of her protective love sheltered him from the consequences of recklessness, irresponsibility and acts of self-indulgence—acts which would have proved the ruin of most professional men.

When she first met him, of course, my mother was completely unaware of the secret impulses and intrinsic weaknesses of his character. In those Victorian days young girls were protected to a somewhat alarming extent from the facts and problems of life. The very word sex was unmentionable, and her innocence enclosed her like a crystal shell. The vitality of this vigorous young man, his warm glances, his ability to cloak a young attractive woman in a radiance of self-esteem, seemed to her unique manifestations for herself alone. When she fell in love with him, as she did soon enough, it did not occur to her to question his facilities or suspect his practised charm.

In his young manhood David Lloyd George was an impressive personality, with many social graces, erect and powerfully built. From photographs and portraits in later life it was popularly believed that he was short in stature. In fact, he was of medium height, about five feet eight inches; it was his unusual masculine development of shoulders and chest that gave the impression of shortness. His head and features, too, even in these days, had a certain leonine quality; the strong brows, the massive sweep of hair, the blue-grey eyes which matched the eloquence and gaiety of his tongue, the strong expressive hands—these were physical attributes calculated to impress almost any feminine heart; and when, allied with these, the young man was already making the imprint of his personality felt in the courts of law and in the councils of local government, a lively respect coloured the admiration. Here was a man it was natural to cherish, and whose easy support of responsible burdens made him worthy of regard.

There was something else that made a strong character like my mother's seek to share the life of this young man. He was poor; he was fighting against odds; he had to make his way ahead on personal merit alone. He would need help, and comfort, and encouragement, and all the things I know it was natural for my mother to give and want to give.

My grandparents—my mother's parents, that is—were soon informed of the courtship. They made their enquiries about David Lloyd George; and they thought the match was unsuitable.

It was no knowledge of his personal weaknesses that brought them to this conclusion, nor indeed his poverty; that he had been brought up by an uncle who was a shoe-maker did not prejudice them against him. They objected to the intended marriage with their daughter for no other reasons than that he was a Baptist and a Liberal with Radical tendencies. It was a religious-political antagonism difficult for us to understand these days; and it was shared by the opposition—that is, by David Lloyd George's uncle and guardian, who contested the Presbyterian-Conservative Owens as doggedly and dogmatically as they opposed him and his.

Maggie Owen was in a serious conflict of loyalties, for the

young man she felt herself to be in love with and for the parents whom she loved. She did not wish to inflict any sort of personal hurt on her parents, or in fact on anyone to whom she was devoted, and the problem became a very real one.

It was then that David Lloyd George showed the early promise of his deftness as a political strategist. Here, indeed, was a situation that he unquestionably enjoyed; opposition—and opposition by the Establishment forces. If the love of Maggie Owen was not enough, opposition by the Establishment certainly was.

He reconnoitred his ground, he examined the findings of Intelligence, he laid his strategic plans and he launched his subtle attack. There was, in fact, a third factor in this contest, this being mainly vested in the person of Maggie Owen's favourite aunt, her father's cousin, Dorothy Roberts, a lady of great character and culture. From the earliest age Maggie Owen had confided all her problems to Aunt Dorothy, whom she regarded as a very wise and good person. There was also a faithful old servant, Margiad, who adored Maggie Owen and for whom the girl had a deep personal attachment.

Lloyd George made repeated visits to Aunt Dorothy. He sought her alliance. He pleaded his case so skilfully and persistently, and touched her romantic heart with such an understanding of its feminine workings, that the lady was quickly and completely won over to the cause of the young lovers, becoming his enthusiastic champion.

As for Margiad, he won her over by the simpler and no less telling technique of involving her in the romantic plot. He engaged her in the rôle of an inarticulate Cyrano, a mute Viola, entrusted to carry love messages backwards and forwards. The service in fact was hardly necessary, as the lovers had hit upon the time-honoured method of the loose brick in the wall, but Lloyd George knew that to involve Margiad in personal service to the cause would stimulate her devotion to it. The eloquent protestations and the fragrant effusions were conveyed with tremulous care by the hand of the faithful elderly cupid.

Lloyd George, hitherto alone, now had two strong allies to exercise their influence on Maggie Owen.

In the meantime, he was successfully warding off a rearguard engagement. His uncle and former guardian, the redoubtable Richard Lloyd and himself no mean hand in the game of personal politics, got down with true Radical-Liberal-Baptist fervour to the task of diverting his nephew's infatuation for the daughter of the house of heretics. In some way that young man could not understand he found himself continually stumbling on unusually comely Welsh maidens of marriageable age. At every turn a blonde or brunette, simpering or meekly smiling, all perfectly happy to be introduced. By an extraordinary coincidence all their antecedents were solid Radical Liberal Baptists to the core. There was, however, only one thing that Lloyd George was more sensitive to than a pretty face, and that was opposition. If anything was calculated to keep him steadily intent on his course it was an attempt at diversionary fire.

Meanwhile Aunt Dorothy was whispering in Maggie Owen's ear words of feminine wisdom about true love being more important than sectarian prejudices and partisan loyalties, that it was a case of the young in heart knowing better than their elders in the long run, and that reconciliation with parents would inevitably follow in the wake of their daughter's assured happiness.

The words thus whispered by a Welsh lady to her niece may well have set the seal on future events that concerned world history, because I am certain that had a lesser woman married Lloyd George he would never have allowed himself the full flowering of his career.

Maggie Owen was all but persuaded to go against her parents' objection, but still she remained undecided, still waited and cogitated, borne on the ebb and flow of conflicting affections.

Two events took place that convinced her that her heart was right. Both concerned my father, and revealed to Maggie Owen the calibre of man he was.

From her private scrap-book, yellow with age, are the cuttings that she kept of events that were significant in her life. One of these concerns a minor court action that took place many years ago in a local court when Lloyd George was a young solicitor who still had to make his way. It told the story of Lloyd George defending four men who had indulged in the traditional local sport of netting salmon. The Chairman of the court—there were six sitting magistrates—a Mr Wynn Griffiths, appeared to be a somewhat apoplectic figure, the terror of young solicitors, who ruled the proceedings with an iron hand and voiced his strictures with a conviction that was not matched by his legal knowledge.

By comparison, the prosecuting solicitor, a Mr Charley Jones, was a mere zephyr breeze lost in the crosswinds of tornado against hurricane.

The hearing was concluded with this dialogue :

Mr George: I again submit that you have not the slightest title of right to try this case, as you have no jurisdiction in the matter.

The Chairman: That question may be finally decided in a superior court.

Mr George: Yes, sir. In a just and unbiased court.

The Chairman: If that remark of Mr George's is meant as a reflection upon any magistrate sitting on this bench I hope that he will name him. A more insulting and ungentlemanly remark to the bench I never heard during the course of my experiences as a magistrate.

Mr George: But a more true remark was never made in a court of justice.

The Chairman (sternly): Tell me to whom you are referring. I must insist upon you to refer to any magistrate or magistrates sitting in this court.

Mr George: Then I refer to you, sir, in particular.

To you, sir, in particular. The words created a local sensation, the young solicitor tweaking the magisterial tiger's whiskers. It was unprecedented. It was foolhardy. It was, in a word, enchanting.

I can well imagine my mother's imagination stirred by this expression of youthful courage. (The magistrates, too, appeared to have been thoroughly disconcerted by it, for the record says that they retired in a body, leaving no instructions about the prisoners, who presumably were left in possession of the arena.)

The other episode was on similar lines, but with additions, embellishments, and demonstrated something beyond courage:

my father's tough-mindedness and formidable legal technique. The story of it fills many pages of my mother's scrap-book and runs to thousands of words. As it has become a *cause célèbre* I will retell it briefly, and as it affected my parents' relationship, deeply touching Maggie Owen's pride in her David.

In 1864 a Mrs Owen (no relative of my mother's) gave a small plot of land as additional burial ground to the Rector of Llanfrothen. No written document supported the bestowal of this gift, but in due course sufficient money was collected to demolish the old boundary wall and build a new one to include and enclose it. In 1880, after the passing of the Burial Acts, the rector strongly objected to the new law that permitted burial services other than those of the Church of England. He persuaded Mrs Owen to execute a deed by which the land she had bestowed was to be used only for burials conducted according to the services of the Church of England.

Some years later a Mr Roberts died, and his executors wished to have him buried with a Nonconformist service beside his daughter in the new part of the cemetery. The rector refused to grant permission, and demonstrated his opposition in a very practical manner. He barred the way for the funeral cortège by padlocking the iron gates.

One of the late Mr Roberts' friends thereupon consulted the young solicitor in Criccieth who had so ably demonstrated his mettle in the magistrates' court.

Mr George acquainted himself with all the facts. He was asked his opinion about the situation and advice what to do.

'Go back,' said Mr George. 'Tear down those gates. Bury your friend beside his daughter, and use whatever service you please.'

Catching some of the spirit of their legal adviser's forthright character, Mr Roberts' friends proceeded to do just that: the gates were forced open and the burial service conducted according to the wishes of the late Mr Roberts.

The rector brought an action for trespass, and legal battle commenced of the sort which Mr George truly relished. In the local court, in spite of the jury's verdict that Mrs Owen had no right under the Statute of Limitations to alter the deed of gift, the judge found the case proved against the defendants. Mr George promptly appealed. He took the case to London, where it was fought out in the High Court of Justice, Mr George's advice was vindicated; their Lordships reversed the decision of the local court, and the appeal with costs to the defendants was allowed.

'*To you, sir, in particular.*'

'*Go back and tear the gates down.*'

Maggie Owen had no need for further proof of the special quality and stature of the man she loved. Such a man was capable of scaling the heights. The fighting morale and moral fervour of the aptly named David in conflict with the authoritarian forces quickened her pride in him, but it did more than that: it revealed to her his vulnerability. It would not always be easy to pierce the cumbersome armour of Goliath with his adroitly aimed sling-shot. There must be times ahead for him when he would be re-jected, perhaps even cast out for his rebelliousness; times when his career, perhaps life itself, might be in danger. (In this her instincts were right, as we shall see.) His need was for more than love. For him inevitably there would be storms ahead, and it was this certainty of his need of her that finally made her over-ride her parents' objection to their marriage.

4

LLOYD GEORGE was now standing at the open door; he was about to enter a new world of national politics. The coming three years—1888 to 1890—were as important as any of his life. On January 24th, 1888, he married Maggie Owen, daughter of Richard and Mary Owen of Mynydd Ednyfed above Criccieth. They lived in this house for the first few years of their married lives. I was born there, in the same room as my mother was born.

On January 17th, 1888, he was twenty-five years of age, and with his mass of dark wavy hair and eloquent, captivating blue-grey eyes he was well equipped for trouble, of a kind my mother never anticipated.

The Local Government Act of 1888 had substituted the new elected County Councils for the old rule by justices, which in practice represented the privileged classes. The Councils had power to grant appointments, and it is a measure of the reputation which Lloyd George enjoyed that at twenty-five he was elected an alderman. A local paper seized on the description, the Boy Alderman, and the name stuck. He remained an alderman of the Caernarvonshire County Council for the rest of his life. His luck was good at the time—explosive and extreme speeches, advocating unconventional views were redeemed by his wit and natural powers of imagery. When he was chosen as the Liberal candidate for parliament one newspaper had this to say, 'He appeared before the constituency under serious disadvantages. He was young and unproved, he had his fortune to make in every sense. He had also brought himself to disfavour by some violent speeches.'

The final effect of these speeches, however, was not unfavour-able. With every fresh impact of his personality his reputation as an original and brilliant advocate increased. His only serious problem was money. His law practice was in its infancy, and apart from the somewhat sensational Llanfrothen case, which had brought him national recognition, there had been nothing outstanding in his legal career to bring him substantial fees. However, such was their faith in his young crusading spirit that the Caernarvon Liberal magnates were willing to dip into their pockets to pay his coming election expenses.

Opportunity came to him when the sitting member, a Conservative, Edmund Swetenham, Q.C., died suddenly on March 19th and caused an immediate by-election in Caernarvon Boroughs.

The Tories were caught somewhat unprepared, and had no special candidate of merit, but eventually decided on Hugh Ellis Nanney, a wealthy landowner, who was by coincidence the squire of my father's own village, Llanystumdwy. He was a kindly-disposed man with no particular flair for politics or public speaking, and laboured under the serious handicap of ignorance of the Welsh tongue. This was a considerable disadvantage when only a minority of the voters were bi-lingual, and all of them imbued with local patriotic fervour. Lloyd George of course could speak both languages with equal facility; in fact, his speeches in Welsh were the more telling and dramatic.

Everything seemed to be going in his favour, and the tide bearing him inexorably towards his greater destiny, when his happy supporters received a major shock that threatened to upset the whole apple-cart. They learned that he had fathered a child on a very charming widow in Caernarvon.

She was not only attractive, but also prominent in social and political circles. There was no question of a planned seduction; it was a mutually light-hearted affair. The young widow was firm and plump and full of sap, with dark red hair and dark brown eyes. They were both members of local musical societies, local amateur theatrical companies. He played Brutus to her Calpurnia; and there were walks in the Welsh hills with the silken nets of fine rain like mists, like ghosts, chased by sun and fragrant wind. There were musical evenings at her home when their voices—my father's was a rich tenor—blended with a singular harmony. These duets, conducted on social and cultural occasions, pro-

41

gressed to closer harmonies and proceeded by stages from the local hall to the private parlour, finding their natural conclusion in the lady's bedroom.

The whole episode was quite characteristic of my father, who, once under the spell of the exercise of his own charm, whether it concerned an audience at a public meeting or consisted of one person, became completely carried away, without any other idea in his head, without a thought of consequences and without the slightest recollection of the family and political responsibilities he carried.

Although these were Victorian days, they were also days of protest against Victorianism. My father was a natural rebel on every level. He was steeped in massive reading about revolutionary times, a devotee of literature concerned with free thought —Charles Bradlaugh, Voltaire, forerunners of Shaw and Wells. The young widow listened and marvelled, and her eyes grew wider. She was an educated woman who was susceptible to the wilful artistry of his ideas. And he had a natural instinct about feminine weakness, as we have seen; he took full account not only of her sensitivity to 'free thought' but to the discontent of her widowed state.

My father was probably the greatest natural Don Juan in the history of British politics, and there seems to be living evidence to prove this. His entire life, including the fifty-three years of marriage with my mother, was involved with a series of affairs with women, some innocent, some romantic, some deeply obsessive, some cynical and worldly, and most of them fruitful. To portray his life without taking into account this side of his personality is like failing to depict Beethoven's handicap of deafness during the composition of his greatest works.

This particular affair with Mrs J. was in the category of a spontaneous overflow of his prodigious energies. At the time my mother was with child (her second infant) and clearly preoccupied with her condition. Her husband felt himself restricted; he was not a man to be confined tamely to the domestic hearth out of a mere sense of marital duty. And the corn was green, and their voices blended. And the widow was willing.

He was brought to a sense of reality with something of a jolt when he found himself with a parliamentary election on his hands, and the knowledge that a whisper of such a scandal would snuff out his career completely and permanently. One can imagine the local bigwigs of the Liberal Party running around in circles to smother the smoke before the fire broke out.

An annuity was obtained for the lady at considerable cost. She had to sign a solemn covenant that nothing should be divulged and that the forthcoming child would never be photographed —otherwise the annuity would be forfeited for ever.

These terms were faithfully observed. I have only once seen my half-brother—I have carefully avoided further contact because the resemblance between us is so strong that for us to be seen together would certainly arouse comment. Sufficient to say that he is a gentleman, unmarried and quite contented in his life and occupation. He would be my twin—though somewhat better nourished, as he can well be with most of the burdens of this world cared for even before his advent into it, and with an appropriately amused view of the workings of fate.

My mother was spared knowledge of the affair—otherwise the shock of such an early flouting of their vows at a time of her pregnancy would have had a disastrous effect on her. She was not to be spared, however, on future occasions, and there were unhappily, many of these. I myself learned about it many years later—there are always people who are willing to acquaint you with the fullest details about a scandal in your own family. They seem even to be prepared to follow you to the ends of the earth in order to do this. I first heard about the Mrs J. affair from a native of Caernarvon whom I stumbled on when I was in South America. We talked over old times and local affairs back home, and then—out it came. 'You knew about your father and Mrs J., of course?' That's how it usually starts, with the pretence that there was nothing deliberate about acquainting you with your father's transgressions. What he told me, even after my longstanding disillusionment, depressed me, saddened and angered me so that I could not rest in my mind until I had either verified the facts or nailed his lies. When I returned to Wales I made enquiries —at the time, this early expression of callousness to my mother seemed black indeed, and perhaps it obsessed me. Unhappily, I learned details that seemed to prove my informant truthful, and when I forced myself to meet my half-brother my last doubts and resistance to the truth were resolved.

Looking back on these events from the perspective of my seventy years of life, I can regard them I think with a certain tranquillity now and, perhaps, even objectivity. My father was a great man, and all who were close to him were inevitably dominated by his stature. His loves, his hates, his angers, his qualities and his weaknesses—they were all exaggerated in our minds, and we lived in their shadow as in the shadow of great events; but today I can see it, I feel, as from a remote hill looking down on my life as on to a valley in which all is plain and the people are small and their actions are not very significant, if not a trifle absurd.

My father's affair with Mrs J. did not survive after the annuity settlement. His interest was more in the conquest than in the relationship itself, and she, an honest enough creature who had recognised clearly the nature of the man she was dealing with from the start, gave no 'trouble'. They continued to meet in public on social occasions, and her attitude to him remained as affable as ever.

Mr George was permitted to continue the pursuit of his career without hindrance.

The election was on April 9th, and the count in Caernarvon on the 10th. His amazing luck still held. The Conservatives were so uncertain of victory that one of their number found it necessary to tip the democratic scales by inserting a bundle of twenty Lloyd George votes into a Nanney file. For the record, my father told me on many occasions that he knew the culprit well, but he would never give his name. The returning officer was about to declare Nanney elected when J. T. Roberts, my father's election agent, demanded a re-count. By some remarkable stroke of good fortune he had been idly flicking the bundles on the table and uncovered twenty Lloyd Georges in the Nanney file.

A re-count gave my father a majority of eighteen.

There seems little doubt that some benign influence was working with the greatest diligence on my father's behalf in order that he should survive the effects both of his own subterfuges and those of Mr Nanney's agent.

The whole county of Caernarvon celebrated the victory that night—with bonfires and torchlight processions. The enthusiasm can well be understood. Here was a poor boy from a humble home, with no privileges of wealth, family or education, measuring swords with the local squire and beating him. A Conservative government was in power at Westminster, and the sitting member whose death had caused the by-election was a Conservative. The victory therefore was all the more remarkable—and having been won by a Welsh-speaking Welshman more than popular; it was a national event.

The torchlight procession bore my father along almost to his front garden that night. I was the innocent cause of putting an end to the celebrations. I was sleeping in my cot when the uninhibited noise of marching and singing men approaching our front gate compelled my mother to send the nurse, Sally, to the front door and demand peace. The vociferations died to a whisper, and the revellers departed on (comparative) tip-toe.

5

THE great adventure for the young Lloyd George began with the first parliamentary-election victory, and the small family moved to London. It was a remarkable experience for the young man, born and raised in the country, to take his place in the 'greatest club in the world' in what was then known as the capital of the universe.

His first day as a 'new boy' coincided with the occasion of a Budget speech, one of the most impressive in the parliamentary calendar; and there, before him, lounging a few yards away, were the great political figures, national personalities whose speeches he had so often studied—even tramped miles across country in order to read—Gladstone, Joe Chamberlain, Lord Randolph Churchill, and the 'uncrowned king of Ireland', Charles Stewart Parnell, the very dramatic storm-centre at the time of a victorious libel suit against no less a journal than *The Times*. He wondered what the Chancellor felt on such an important day as he saw the dispatch box unlocked for the revelation of profound financial secrets. But on the whole he refused to be over-awed, recalling that every one of them had felt as though his mouth were full of coal dust when delivering his maiden speech.

There were several weeks before the Whitsun recess, and he decided not to rush forward into battle on this strange terrain. He would spend the time studying the personalities, the character of his audience, the dry, austere and witty Speaker, who ruled the proceedings; above all, he was determined to master the rules of procedure, because this was a strange, two-edged weapon which had often flummoxed an over-confident would-be orator. In fact, it was eight weeks before he took the plunge and made his maiden speech, a restrained, appropriately modest address on a subject on which he was an expert. The speech did not set fire to the Thames; that was not its purpose. He held himself well in hand, spoke fluently and good-humouredly, matching the casual air of the most hard-bitten audience in the land, which had the keenest ear for pompousness and the keenest eye for inflated ego.

The usual kindly and courteous reception was accorded this first and very promising speech. But henceforward there would be no mercy.

The subject on which he chose to address the House was an amendment to a Bill to compensate publicans whose licences became redundant. Not a very inspiring subject, it would appear; but Lloyd George saw the hidden implications—the pampering of a relatively affluent section of the community. As far as his constituency was concerned the money would be far better spent on improving educational facilities. Such arguments by the nationalist Welsh members were familiar enough to his audience, who were far more interested in the way these arguments would be presented. They listened critically and appreciatively—the young man had poise, precision; and they were conscious of hidden power under control which indicated an early maturity.

Lloyd George was not inactive outside the House. He made speeches in the Midlands during these early weeks, before more familiar types of audiences; and these were not sophisticated, facty expositions, but unchecked bursts of eloquence which worked on the emotions of his listeners—the style of address that really suited him and of which he was quickly becoming a master. These, too, were reported in the Press, and clearly indicated his early ability to rivet mass audiences.

Thus he began his apprenticeship in the national arena.

At home in London, the Lloyd Georges lived modestly, with a careful eye on expenditure. In those days, Members of Parliament received no salary. Lloyd George had saved a little from his law practice, which was now being carried on quite successfully by his younger brother, William (Uncle Lloyd helping out as 'managing clerk'); and undoubtedly his national reputation was drawing ever more clients to the firm which bore his name. Uncle William was one of those quiet, loyal characters, totally free from envy, who was content to stay in the back seat. There were several such devoted allies in Lloyd George's career. My mother's family would have helped in financial matters without question, but my father showed early a complete desire for independence. He turned down with scorn a nominal directorship in an Oxford Street firm which would have supplemented his earnings handsomely. 'A guinea-pig director? No—it has not yet come to this!' He did a hard journalistic stint on a freelance basis and earned a few guineas by this means.

My parents made the acquaintance of successful Welsh 'migrants'—drapers in Oxford Street, who had founded famous firms, bankers and insurance underwriters. Peter Jones, D. H. Evans, John Lewis—these are household names today, of course. It was an elect colony of Welshmen; but by their standards, my father was as poor as a church mouse in those days. No matter; he held his head high. He was accepted; and friendships or acquaintanceships endured for very many years.

In the House, too, there were several good friends and allies— Tom Ellis and other Welsh nationalists, particularly Sam Evans, with whom my father formed a memorable filibuster combination (which I shall describe later) that made its first major impact for him in Parliament.

And of course he discovered the London theatre! Beerbohm Tree was his favourite. And how eagerly the orator studied the art of the stage performer—timing, modulation of voice, gesture —and to what admirable effect he put them. Even in those early days, my father was rapidly becoming for me a sort of wonder man, a mesmerist, a story-teller who could enact the rôles of six different characters from Monte Cristo or David Copperfield. This was his method of introducing me to literature—as we were a Welsh-speaking family, he was at great pains to see that we children knew just what we would be missing if we did not master the language of our adopted country. Thus I wept bitterly over Mr Murdstone's cruelty to poor helpless David. And when Jean Valjean put his mighty shoulder under the shaft of the broken cart to release the guard slowly being pulverised beneath it, I held my breath until my face turned scarlet in sympathy with the strain; and my father would have to terminate the performance abruptly to prevent me having convulsions.

When I was a child, my father was almost invariably kind and gentle. He shared the male characteristic with his family in being

48

Lloyd George at the Opening of Parliament, February 1914.

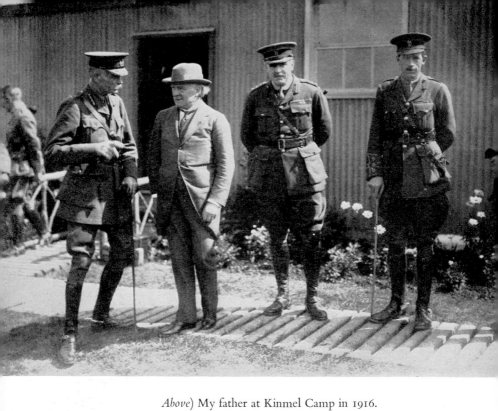

Above) My father at Kinmel Camp in 1916.

(*Below*) With the King and the Prince of Wales at Victoria Station, June 1919.

unable to inflict chastisement on the children. The male members of the household left these unpleasant duties to the womenfolk. (I was the same as a parent.) I sometimes got a smacking from my mother, and whenever I was due to receive it, my father ducked out of the room.

I have no real memory of our first London home, which was in Essex Court, near the Strand. We moved rather frequently in our first years in London, my mother being always restless when she was away from Criccieth; but all our homes were comfortable, very well run and invariably staffed by Welsh servants. There was a rather strange contrast in our lives as a result: as soon as we stepped outside the house we were in a foreign land— with a different language, customs and mental climate. It was always a great relief to return home from this foreign country, and I am sure that at the first sound of our warm Welsh tongue we all felt an easing of tension, particularly in the very terrible days of strain we all suffered during my father's anti-war period in the Boer campaign.

During his early months in London my father had an adventure of which I later was to receive a memorable account. The East End of London was being terrorised by the psychopath killer, Jack the Ripper, and with the same love of action which the young Winston Churchill showed some years later in the Sidney Street 'siege', father volunteered to join a police superintendent in a hunt for the murderer. He joined forces with other colleagues in Aldgate, and they set off to track the dark wilderness of one of the worst slum regions in the world virtually by torchlight—beyond Central London, the street lighting was almost non-existent.

'And did you find any trace of the Ripper?' I asked him.

'I found something worse. Something that Dante's pen alone could describe. Within a hundred yards of sanity and civilisation, a million people lived in conditions that gave the Ripper's actions a character of mercy killings. The gin houses; the doss houses; the stinking alleys and the gruesome cellars; the rickety tenements; the disorderly houses and the thieves' dens. This was London, the capital of the greatest Empire the world has ever known, the centre of the richest country in the world. I set out to investigate a crime that night; I found evidence of ten thousand.'

I think that night's experience completed my father's Radical education.

I find a record of an early storm in the House of Commons, whipped up by the young Lloyd George at about this time, over what would normally have been a routine supplementary estimate to cover the cost of a royal pageant. One of the items was a fee of about £450 to bestow a title on Prince Henry of Prussia. L. G. pointed out that this honour—Knight of the Garter—was granted for exceptional service to the country. Now what did Prince Henry ever do for this country?—or, for that matter, for his own country? (Scandalised exclamations by his interrupters.) There was another item of £180 in respect of the Duchess of Cambridge's funeral. Why should this private function be put to the expense of the national exchequer? (Horror.) From first to last *that ducal family had received three million pounds from public funds.* (Abashed silence at last.) Having established his hearing, Lloyd George moved in to the atttack. And with what splendid broadsides he chastised the painfully embarrassed Members! He gave them the plain facts of social injustice in a manner they had never before heard in the House, quoting chapter and verse from the report of the Enquiry into Sweated Labour. In the years that followed the House listened abashed to many passionate appeals that caused heart-searching and doubt whether, after all, all was for the best in the best of all possible worlds. From Keir Hardie; from the young Ramsay MacDonald; from Philip Snowden; from Jimmy Maxton and Willie Gallacher; from Nye Bevan. But the first challenge, the first appeal came from the solitary voice of Lloyd George.

He was to make his stand on issues of poverty and social injustice in the years to come, and the most concrete achievements of his statesmanship were the foundations of the welfare state and social services as we know them today; and this early speech was a foretaste of the future which had a very strong and exotic flavour on the palates of his listeners.

In his early period in the House, however, he was mainly interested with questions that concerned Wales. There was the Disestablishment issue—out with the English Church! A land commission—out with the squires and gamekeepers! And more money for education, please. These were good, hard, fighting issues of a practical kind, which he championed in a way that made the House recognise a formidable Welsh clansman in their midst —knowledgeable, voluble, irrepressible, rumbustious. Even his leader, Gladstone (who was otherwise delighted with him), found him hard to handle as, even in those very early days, he would not accept Party discipline readily. In fact, the only discipline he ever supported was that imposed by himself—clearly he never had the makings of a follower. Either he would lead or fall. It was not long before he led the Welsh members—and not content with that, he had a new policy—Home Rule for Wales! (The Irish wanted it. What was good enough for Parnell was good enough for Lloyd George.)

'Home Rule for Ireland? Yes. And Home Rule for Scotland? Why not? Home Rule for Wales? Certainly. And Home Rule even for England!' he conceded graciously.

'How about Home Rule for Hell?' interposed a tired voice from the back benches.

'Agreed. Let every man speak for his own country.'

On the whole, over this issue of Welsh independence he succeeded in frightening his followers rather more than the opposition. Home Rule for Wales was something quite new, a personal pet of Mr Lloyd George's. Nobody seriously wanted to be cut off from the industrial power and markets of Great Britain and her Empire, except the obstinate Irish patriots who cared as much for practical issues as poets care for the Civil Service. He soon found himself alone on this question, and let it die a natural death.

I am sure he never seriously intended to carry it through. Many years later when he was Prime Minister, with a dominant position in the Cabinet and a large majority in the House, he made not the slightest attempt to realise this early policy, this patriotic dream; and I remember once asking him rather cynically, 'What would old Abe Lincoln have said about this secession programme of yours?'

He had the grace to chuckle.

'Well, what do you say?' I insisted.

'I pass.'

Those were days of plain speaking and good-humoured invective—almost a lost art in Parliament now. One of the most memorable feuds was between L. G. and the Anglican Bishop of St Asaph. They were most delectably rude to one another and formed such a respect for the other's Johnsonian prowess that they finished up by becoming great friends. The Bishop referred to the Nonconformists as 'shrivelled, meagre, lewd and troublesome insects'. 'No doubt he passed his examinations,' countered Lloyd George, referring to the Bishop's modest intellectual gifts, 'But you cannot even make a first-rate bishop out of a third-rate scholar, a fifth-rate preacher and an irate priest.' At a meeting in Flintshire, the chairman, introducing the guest speaker, Mr Lloyd George, said, 'I have to present to you the Member for Caernarvon Boroughs, who has come here to reply to what the Bishop of St Asaph said the other night about Welsh Disestablishment. In my opinion, ladies and gentlemen, the Bishop of St Asaph is one of the biggest liars in Crrreashon, but thank God, we have in Mr Lloyd George a match for him tonight!'

6

I WAS a child at the time.

Parents quarrelling can be one of the personal tragedies of children.

I heard voices at night. Father's. Deep, unrecognisably harsh, dominating. And mother's, anguished, close to hysteria.

I listened—groping my way out of sleep, into reality, into consciousness that I had not been dreaming.

I don't know how I summoned the courage to go into the room where my parents were conducting some terrible adult rite. I stood, fogged and dazzled by the light, hearing my voice raised in an imperious childish treble, 'Don't hurt mamie!'

The silence that followed was like smashing glass. My father, who had loomed up before me, stopped, hesitated, flinched as though I had hurt him; and then he turned away from me. He turned away and stood with his back to me——

It was difficult for me to understand his doing this—flinching from my words, my childish demand. He seemed to have become diminished somehow, grown smaller. He would not face his accuser. I wanted an explanation from him, an assertion of authority. Was this the marvellous superman, my father? Flinching from me and turning his back. Why hadn't he denied he was hurting mother?

On this occasion mother picked me up with fierce tenderness and hurried me back to bed. No explanation for the parental quarrel was given me at the time and, childish memory being mercifully brief, the next day everything seemed to be normal once more. It was put out of mind. For the time being.

I remember 'visiting' with father. It was the home of Welsh friends, my parents' social circle in London. I was playing happily amongst the furniture in the drawing-room, examining pictures and the tortoise-shell inlay of the escritoire. Father and the lady of the house were alone with me. They seemed very absorbed in each other.

Then father began to play some sort of silly game with the lady. He seemed to be eating her fingers.

'Dick, do you like fruit?' the lady said to me.

'Of course he does,' father said.

'There are some nice plum and apple trees in the garden,' the lady said. 'Why don't you go and gather some fruit. It's delicious.'

'Yes, all right.'

Off I went; but being a well brought up little boy I selected some of the ripest fruit for our hostess.

I returned with my gift a little sooner than they expected, and my interruption was not welcome. Nobody seemed to appreciate my carefully selected ripe plums.

'Did you have a nice time?' mother asked me later, when we returned home.

'Oh, yes. I had a scrumptious tea. Then I picked some fruit. Father and Mrs D. were playing a game. He was eating her hand, and they didn't want any fruit.'

'*Dic bach*, go and play in your room.'

'But——'

'Don't argue.'

I wandered off. As soon as the door closed I began to hear the voices.

One of the worst quarrels followed father's holiday in South America. He wrote marvellous letters which mother read to us. They were gay, romantic, colourful. He was in the Argentine, amongst the mountains and glens, the peons and sunsets and thunderstorms. Father loved adventure and described a journey on horseback on the narrow mountain passes, lit by flashes of lightning, blindly allowing the mount his head and trusting his surefootedness. His guides preceded him, twanging their guitars.

It appeared, however, that this was not the only romantic adventure he enjoyed in that part of the world. When he came home there was another quarrel, this one more violent than I had ever known. At one point we were visited by his friend and partner, Rhys Roberts, who acted as a sort of mediator or arbitrator.

I remember confronting him as he left my parents' room. 'Mr Roberts, why are they shouting? It's horrible when they quarrel—— Why do they do it? Can't you stop them? It's awful—I can't bear to listen——'

He took my arm. 'It's not your mother's fault, Dick. Your father's been rather a bad lad. He's headstrong and spoiled and his head's too easily turned. But it will be all right. Your mother is very sensible and understands him thoroughly.'

When father returned from Buenos Aires my childish susceptibilities received a shock. He had shaved off his luxuriant moustache—a physical attribute of which he had been justifiably proud. This transformed him in such a way that we children suffered considerable anxiety about his true identity. Was it really father? He seemed like a stranger to us, and even after all these years I can recall backing away from him when he first greeted me on his return.

The episode began to have significance when I learned the reason for this change in him. In Buenos Aires the members of the small party of English travellers, which included Sir Henry Dalziell, were invited into many homes and had warm Latin hospitality lavished on them. Father was as popular as ever and it appeared that, even with his little knowledge of Spanish, he was able to make himself perfectly well understood in a more universal language. No doubt his personality never really needed linguistic embellishments—his physical charms, his natural grace, his wicked glance were quite enough for most women.

There was a Spanish lady, married to a successful business man, with the romantic Christian name, I believe, of Dolores. I have not the least doubt that father found her Latin ways and personality exotic; and to her this equally exotic stranger, who combined the poise of an Englishman with the warmth of temperament of his Welsh antecedents, appeared irresistible.

I cannot from this remote date recall the details that I later learned about their affair, except that it almost finished in tragedy. The lady's husband found out about it and father hastened to take cover in an obscure hotel. Dire Latin threats resounded through the city and there was a danger that gunshots might sound amidst the castanets and twanging guitars.

The outraged husband issued a challenge. A duel, swords or pistols; father was given his choice of weapons.

I think that if he had been a bachelor and independent professional man, he would not have shirked even this encounter—his thirst for personal experience and adventure was pretty insatiable —but he had his family to consider, and his career in Parliament, and the noise of the scandal was so ominous that had it been allowed to develop in the form of a duel with bloodshed, it would have immediately echoed across the Atlantic.

'What shall we do?' father asked his friends. 'I daren't step out of the hotel.'

It was true; the husband had hired sleuths to track him down.

'We'll have to have that moustache off,' Sir Henry told father with solemn humour. 'It's a dead give-away.'

'My moustache—never!'

Father defended this Edwardian embellishment with a Samson-like tenacity; but in the end he realised that it was either his whiskers or ruin.

Protesting to the end, he removed his upper growth; and they managed to smuggle him out of the country, shorn but intact.

He did not, however, allow for feminine perspicacity when he returned home. He discovered that this act of camouflage was, to my mother, also a 'dead give-away'. She knew that he would never have parted with his whiskers except at pistol point and none of his explanations for doing so gave her the slightest satisfaction.

With true wifely persistence and indefatigable feminine suspicion, she pursued the explanations until inevitably he made some revealing remark which she seized upon. It was, then, a woman.

In any case the moustacheless Lloyd George had caused a stir on his return home, and the story had been brought back from across the seas, quite understandably, as a choice tit-bit. It was all over town, in the clubs and drawing-rooms; Fleet Street caught echoes of it and mother learned all the facts.

He seemed to have no genuine reason for these extra-marital pastimes. He was as much as ever in love with my mother. She was certainly a very handsome woman, and a mental match for him, capable of giving him companionship in the fullest sense. Why did he indulge in these amorous sports?

The truth was that father had almost no ordinary interests outside his work. He was no socialite like Curzon; he was no gourmet like Mond; he had no expert appreciation of a bottle of wine like Winston; he was not a sportsman like Rosebery. He had only one form of recreation, which he followed all the years of his adult life. Marriage had nothing to do with it; and his adventures were kept in separate watertight compartments for the most part—if he were found out, it was through no intention of his own.

And when he was found out he would behave more like a child than an adult. There would be a lot of bluster and protest until it was clear that this would avail him nothing; and then he would adopt his hurt manner, assuring mother that she was the only woman he had ever really loved, that he relied on her completely; and what would happen to him if she left him? She was his guide and refuge. He would sink into decline. His career would be cut off at its prime. Whether he believed these protests or not it is impossible to say; but my mother believed them, and as events proved, she was right.

In the meanwhile, he carried on, adventure following adventure, with many hair's-breadth escapes. For years he remained unscathed, protected by his wife from the consequences of his excesses.

I met socially quite a number of his partners in gallantry over the years, many of whom belonged to the Welsh circle in London, and the 'bohemian' set, of which father was very fond. Nothing gave him greater pleasure than an evening of entertainment amongst professional performers, sopranos, young actresses of distinction, famous beauties, artists and their friends. Many of them came to listen to him in the House, sitting in the Strangers' Gallery and enjoying his performances as though they were at the theatre listening to Irving. As soon as he finished, the Gallery would empty itself as though the management had announced an outbreak of fire. I am sure they recognised a kindred spirit, a fellow artist.

He was an attractive man, capable of playing to the gallery if he had a mind to. He was an intellectual, but he could amuse a child for an hour; and he had only to wish it and he could charm and fascinate the most exalted beauty of his day. But, as if it were not enough that he should be irresistible to women, he found *them* irresistible. He was pushed and pulled simultaneously in the same direction.

I have heard a friend at a party say to his companion (a most assured beauty), 'That's Lloyd George. The shortish man in the group over there.'

'Don't be silly,' she replied. 'I can see from here he's eight feet tall.'

In fact, even if he was the shortest man in the group, he was invariably the centre of it; and I would watch with amusement, making side-bets with myself, how quickly the old man and the most attractive females in the gathering gravitated to each other. The effect they had on each other was fascinating to watch. A woman who with you had seemed stilted, frigid, inarticulate, so that you were racking your brain to try to find things to say to her, the moment she found herself in father's presence, became gracious, witty, vivacious.

As far as preference was concerned, his tastes seemed to be remarkably catholic, which is putting it euphemistically. I have always assumed that women, like wine, should be chosen for quality. Father recognised no such restrictions. There were beauties by the dozen in his life, but he would happily ring the changes on the oddest selection of nondescript types. I suppose that in some way or other almost any female presented a challenge, like the nun to Don Juan; and it is possible that he had the power to invoke certain hidden qualities in them in the way a connoisseur can detect a masterpiece in an old faded canvas.

I remember sitting in a restaurant with him through which passed cohorts of fashionable, handsome creatures. A most statuesque enchantress passed our table, conscious of being the centre of masculine attention, dipping and swaying like a yacht with all its sails engaged.

I made some youthfully appreciative remark; but father hardly raised his eyes from his soup plate. 'Handsome. Like one of Rosebery's fillies. And about as exciting,' was his indifferent comment.

Another queen of the follies passed by a little later, all pink and white perfection.

'I've lost my taste for sugar mice,' father said a little testily after another effusion of praise from me.

Then, a little later, a pale, dark-eyed woman, in her late thirties, her hair in a severe unfashionable bun, appeared; and father sat up and watched her lingeringly as she passed, otherwise unnoticed, to some obscure table.

'Now, she's *interesting*,' he said. 'She has something. She's a deep one, I'll wager.'

He leaned forward confidentially and I waited, my ears at the alert—but then, becoming aware of our relationship, he sat back and addressed himself to his pressed duck.

We were strolling in St James' Park one day with one of his Welsh friends. A very attractive woman passed us, and father leaned back on his cane to watch her appraisingly.

'Now that's dangerous,' his friend said. 'You've so many notches on that cane, George, it's a miracle it doesn't collapse under you.'

They both roared; and even my untutored youthful mind did not fail to appreciate the point of the joke.

He was excessively virile. Combining brains with so much physical prowess, his women friends built a legend round him to which he clung even in the years of his dotage. In the end it made him a pathetically foolish figure; but there is no doubt that in his youth and middle age he was a redoubtable womaniser.

There would be little need to illustrate this facet of his character but for the fact that it explains the sudden decline of the statesman and political crusader at a relatively early age, but this tragic chapter I shall write later.

Like most very virile men he had a special tenderness for the female sex. His exquisite love for my sister Mair, much of which was later transferred after her death to Megan, was remarked by all our friends. And, again, like most virile men, he had a certain feminine strain of subtlety that made him understand them thoroughly, enjoy every form of intercourse with them, mental as well as physical.

'A woman is said to have a mind like a grasshopper,' he said to me once. 'Don't believe it. She has a mind like a butterfly. Its erratic progress is a form of protectiveness. And so pretty.'

And another time: 'A woman's emotional nature is like a Bach fugue, difficult to understand, difficult to follow, but wonderfully rewarding to those willing to concentrate.'

My parents' friends amongst the Welsh colony included a successful draper and his wife. I remember the lady quite well. She was a lively, attractive creature, rather loquacious, very stylish, perhaps a little flamboyant as I recall.

There were Sunday outings—I was ten or eleven at the time and I remember father taking me for long walks in the country around Walham Green. Although still so young, nevertheless I was already aware that these country excursions, in the company of father and Mrs D., had a purpose that was not really innocent. I was encouraged to go ahead and to play with the younger children and I sensed that it was a deliberate move on father's part. I strongly resented the idea that I was being used, with the other children, to provide cover for their *tête-à-tête*. These early suspicions had been encouraged by my unusually precocious initiation into the transgressions of adults.

The affair with Mrs D. continued for longer than most of father's gallantries and it was memorable to me because of the cynical way in which he exploited his own influence in order to further it. Mr D., although quite a good business man and trades-man, was a colourless personality. He had, however, certain ambitions which I think would have remained unfulfilled were it not for father's assistance.

Mr D. wanted a social and parliamentary career. That he had little real talent or distinction did not prove a hindrance when Lloyd George was ready to exert his influence to help him. Father got him into the House by helping him in his election campaign, appearing on the platform frequently as his spokesman. In due course, when he was in a position to do so, he awarded Mr D. a government post.

The affair with Mrs D. flourished under cover for many years. They had many opportunities to meet on social occasions; and long before my mother was sure of the situation, I had formed my own conclusions about it. The lady was amiable enough and went out of her way to be friendly, but my youthful hostility—and there is no more rigorous moralist than a small child—made me repel every one of her rather kindly overtures. I thought she was very attractive and she wore a fragrance like a basket of carnations; but none of her blandishments were proof against my inarticulate and tightly-contained antagonism.

Whether or not Mrs D. recognised the reason for my childish hostility I cannot be certain; but she went out of her way to be pleasant. She even remembered that I had expressed a wish to read a certain popular schoolboy novel that had appeared in a lavish illustrated edition. Just before my birthday she handed me the volume, neatly tied with ribbon. I accepted it very self-consciously, blushing and stammering my thanks automatically.

I took it up to my room later that day and examined it with care, dwelling a long time on the bright illustrations with all their promise of a feast of adventure. Ritualistically, and with school-boy solemnity, I carefully tore out the middle and end chapters of the book, page by page, and then destroyed them. Thus I had saved myself from the temptation of enjoying Mrs D's gift. . . .

Mrs D. had three children and either the second or third child —I cannot now recall which—bore the same name as one of my sisters; and later when the affair became known to my mother, this represented one of her deeper feminine grievances.

Needless to say Lloyd George's wife found out about this long after the facts became generally known to her social set. There was a lot of gossip about it at the time and a friend of mine later told me that Mrs D. had admitted to him that one of her children was the issue of her association with Lloyd George. I was still young enough to be vastly shocked by this disclosure; and unfortunately I had little reason to doubt its truth in the light of subsequent events.

7

MY father used to campaign up and down the country, staying with political friends or distant relatives. He was considerably sought after as a guest—young, witty, entertaining, personable, highly-publicised always in the districts where he spoke. All his life he was flattered by those who felt themselves encircled in the aura of success which he radiated; and amongst these were women, countless women, bored with their relatively humdrum lives, who seized the opportunity to bask in a little temporary reflected glory through their association with him; and I do not underestimate his personal qualities of persuasion —he could charm a bird of paradise into the net.

In July '97, there appeared a divorce petition, Edwards against Edwards, who cited a co-respondent, Wilson; and Mrs Edwards, who was a distant relative of my mother's and defendant in the suit, confessed to misconduct with another man, referred to as A.B. The document she signed, however, stated that on the 4th February, 1896, she committed adultery with Lloyd George, M.P., and that the 'said Lloyd George is the father of the child, and that I have on previous occasions committed adultery with the above Lloyd George.'

Catherine Edwards, my mother remembered, was a pretty, pert, amiable young woman at the time, with a carefree disposition. On the night in question—the 4th February—her husband, who was a doctor, had been called away from home on a case, and it was alleged that my father, a guest staying under his roof, took advantage of his absence to make love to his wife.

It was a grave accusation—bad enough at any time—and in those days, fatal to the career of a public man, if substantiated.

The child referred to, however, had been born in August—and there was no evidence that it was a premature birth; so that if conceived, the occasion must have been an earlier one than on the date specifically referred to. And to refute the charge my father was able to produce a record of his attendance in the House of Commons on the 4th February, until early in the morning—the Edwards lived in Montgomeryshire, and, thus, clearly the young woman's confession was inaccurate at least in its reference to that particular act of misconduct.

How she came to sign this 'confession'; how she was persuaded to do so—or whether it was a piece of feminine aberration—it is, of course, impossible for me to say. Had it been an isolated accusation, I would not even refer to it. As everyone knows, women sometimes indulge in fantasies about affairs with public men, and many a popular personality has been annoyed by un-warranted charges of this sort from neurotic women, some of whom have sued for paternity costs. Unfortunately, in my father's career of gallantry, there were too many of these episodes to sup-port this theory.

Divorce lawyers on both sides were persuaded not to make any further reference to the 'confession' which was solemnly with-drawn from the file of documents at the hearing—in any case, there was quite enough evidence against the lady to secure the objective sought. Therefore the awkward question as to where he was on the 'previous occasions' referred to in her statement was left forever in obscurity. The comfortable supposition was that her fabrication had been designed to shield another man.

My father's chief safeguard in these affairs was that he was almost never seriously involved emotionally—mainly, they were tran-sient adventures. He had no sense of loyalty to his mistresses, and could present a bold, indignant front, with flat protestations that he was being 'victimised by these vainglorious harpies, who wanted to boast of their conquest of me'. These protestations and equivocations did not long deceive my mother, nor anyone else closely connected with him. However, there was almost never any continuing association, so that at any particular time he could declare without fear of contradiction, 'Hardly know the woman. Haven't seen her for months and have not the least intention of seeing her again.'

63

At the time, however, father had a bad fright and it needed all his gifts of histrionics to convince my mother that this was mere 'fantasy on poor crazy Catherine's part'.

Poor, crazy Catherine. That name must have given my father many an ironic twinge.

Another Catherine—a charming, beautiful and talented one—had also been involved in a divorce scandal that had rocked the Irish idol, Charles Stewart Parnell, off his throne. And the injustice of it was that with these two the love affair was a genuine one.

My father knew Parnell, of course; and early in his career he dined with him and sympathetically discussed the Irish leader's grave personal problem which was having a devastating effect on his career. Roman Catholic Ireland, Victorian England and Nonconformist Wales were deeply shocked by Captain O'Shea's successful divorce petition which cited Parnell. Gladstone—dear old Mr Gladstone, 'bless him, may hell be hot for him' as Richard Aldington wrote—sent a letter to the Irish group that he could not support their Home Rule policy if Parnell retained their leadership. John Morley and the Irish nationalists held a meeting to decide future policy and the possible effects of this ultimatum. It was a bitter affair. John Redmond demanded whether Parnell or Gladstone were Master of the Irish Party, leaving himself wide open, of course, to Healy's retort, 'And who is to be Mistress of the Party?'

Parnell became virtually estranged from all his colleagues, but my father, to his credit, said to him one evening, 'Come and let me introduce you to a Welsh friend who wishes to meet you.'

'Ah,' said Parnell, smiling for the first time for many days, 'I did not know I had a friend left in Wales.'

I think the evening my father spent with Parnell on that occasion must have been a most melancholy and ironic one. He said later that Parnell's error had been a tactical one in not resigning from the leadership before the divorce was heard. This would have stolen Gladstone's thunder and kept Parnell at least within the ranks of the Irish Party in the House, where he could re-emerge naturally as its leader in due course—in practice he would have retained the leadership inevitably, and when the scandal was forgotten, he would be restored as its official leader.

But I think the error was not a tactical one. I think the mistake he made was to love a woman truly, stand by her loyally, and openly and honestly declare his love.

8

HAVING well accustomed himself to the procedure of the House, got the 'feel' of his audience, mastered the tactics of deployment and obstruction that characterise the expert parliamentarian, Lloyd George eagerly awaited his opportunity for a trial of strength and skill.

It came with the Tithe Recovery Bill. This was a subject on which Lloyd George was an expert. He and Sam Evans formed a filibuster combination which practically broke the nerve of the opposition by its persistence, suppleness, flexibility of defence and endless, untiring pressure. They fought each line of the Bill for months, speaking alternately seven or eight times a day till the small hours of the morning. As amendment after amendment was rejected so they framed new ones, or what appeared to be new ones, until their opponents realised that the 'new' amendments had exactly the same purpose as the ones rejected, only more so. Lloyd George was young and strong, revelling in opposition, enjoying the contest as well as he ever loved a good argument in the smithy. He wore them down and wore them down until the first crack appeared—and then he and Sam Evans began to pull their punches. They did not really want the Bill thrown out! They only wanted to bend it a little.

This they did admirably—with nearly half their amendments incorporated. The veterans resisting them had seldom had such a shaking up; the most eminent London lawyers exchanged looks of astonishment at the adroitness with which the country boy from Caernarvon handled subtle legal points in the framing of riders and qualifications. And his marathon technique was intimidating.

I think that this was the basis of my father's genius: his superb application and single-minded concentration when his interest in a public matter was deeply involved—no detail was too small to be studied, no reference too obscure to be noted, and nothing was big enough to frighten him—no convention, opposition or other obstacle. This ability to see with double vision—in breadth and horizon, a hawk's view—and in close-up detail, with the clinical eye of a microscope—forged his technique of greatness in Parliament. Other men had been great orators, who could make the broad sweeping declamations that swayed emotion; other men had been formidable 'committee' experts, who could array in meticulous order the scattered filings of reference so that they became magnetised in orderly parade, north and south, the lot of them, marching like ants. But this combination of qualities— orator and committee expert—was a rare, almost unique phenomenon. Since Pitt and Cromwell, I doubt whether there has been anyone to match Lloyd George.

It has been said he never was a committee man, that he hated committees, ignored them or overrode them; but this is to mistake the form for the substance. When his interests were engaged, he adopted a pure committee technique—provided he sat on it alone. But this was not mere egotism. He just could not bother with second-hand opinions. Sitting alone, he was in the midst of forty dozen tomes of reference, happily burrowing and collecting ammunition for his oratorical howitzer, packing it very compact in the chamber.

Take the second important occasion of his early parliamentary career—the Agricultural Land Rating Bill. Here was something that looked like dry bones to the conventional orator—rating laws, rents, capital values, land assessments. The government had brought in the Bill with a most plausible air that its intent was to relieve the working farmers; and the run of the mill member would impatiently accept the findings and figures of government valuation experts. Lloyd George not only refused to accept these findings, he set about to prove that the consequence of the Bill would have the opposite effect claimed, that of helping the landlord; and further, he even submitted that honourable members of the government would themselves be beneficiaries under this proposed Bill, and showed to what extent, in hard cash, such benefits would mean to them individually.

He went on fighting the Bill with the same fiendish relish and persistence that he had showed over Tithes, the other question of which he had made himself a master. He fought and he fought. 'Has Lloyd George been speaking all the morning?' 'Lloyd George *still* speaking?' 'Hasn't anyone but Lloyd George spoken?' (This from a report in the hostile *Western Mail*, unconsciously paying tribute to him, referring to questions asked by slightly punch-drunk members who had left the House worn out by the indefatigable oratory of the Member for Caernarvon Boroughs, and on their return, some hours later, still found him on his feet.)

This of course is great stuff. The reader will be surprised, perhaps, to note that there were other occasions when Lloyd George was unable to utter a word on the simplest of topics. I remember an occasion in the House—I was in the Gallery at the time—when the Speaker in vain tried to catch *his* eye, as he had been expected to make a tribute to the King of the Belgians. He sat mute, a sheet of paper clutched in a paralysed grip in his hand; and after an astonished pause that embarrassed the House, a friend quickly rose and eased the atmosphere by deputising for him in a short, moving address. And only an hour ago, over lunch, father had run through some of the points he confidently expected to make that afternoon. I asked him about his 'freeze' later, and he smiled and said that this sort of thing did sometimes happen even to the most experienced speaker—stage fright is a phenomenon that persists throughout one's entire life, and the more sensitive the artist the greater the tension in the wings.

'Had I been able to get up, I would have been all right. I knew exactly what I wanted to say; my tongue and brain knew their business—they had had their instructions. But I had forgotten to issue similar orders to my knee joints.'

These occasions of course were exceedingly rare in my father's case, and although the incident at the time was a rather painful one, looking back on it now I find it one that seems rather endearing. These touches of humanity, after all, bring the great men down to the level of us ordinary mortals.

The thoroughness with which Lloyd George applied himself in these days (and later) often exhausted itself in his speeches. In other matters, he was persistently inefficient and hopelessly dilatory. I have mentioned that he was the world's worst correspondent (except for a daily letter to Uncle Lloyd right through his career). His study was swamped with shoals of *unopened* letters; the unanswered ones would fill a museum. The pockets of his coat bulged with correspondence from all over the country— these were the letters specially selected as being superior in importance to the ones left strewn about the floor under his desk but they invariably shared a similar fate, because when there was no more room in his bulging pockets for new additions to the 'file', he would simply empty them into a desk drawer where they would turn yellow in their envelopes. When someone had the temerity to reproach him about keeping correspondents waiting indefinitely, he would reply, with disarming sophistry, that by now the letters had answered themselves. In fact, he was a great man for essentials. For what he believed to be really necessary no effort was spared, but from the early days of his career he would have needed half a dozen secretaries to cope with enquiries from constituents, the Press, Welsh nationalists, cranks and all sorts. But the habit of not answering letters, thus formed, persisted in later life when he had all the secretarial help anyone ever needed. It has been said that some correspondents who wanted a plain and simple answer to a query, would enclose two postcards, stamped and addressed, one bearing the word Yes and the other No. The old man would then exercise his boyish sense of mischief and return both cards to their sender.

And unless he himself considered something to be important, he was quite unable to deal with it. In later life, poor, harassed, splendid Sylvester, his official secretary—who had given up wonderful opportunities to serve sane men—would follow him about for hours, shorthand notebook and pen in hand, to catch him off guard and trap him into an answer to some query. He was the bane of his ministerial assistants, who were tied in knots trying to get a decision from their chief. He would regard them mischievously and challenge them to make one of their own— 'and see it's the right one. Any fool can make a wrong decision'. I think that in a minor sense, and a purely mental one, he was something of a sadist. When confronted with a situation which interested him or which he considered important, decisions rattled out of him like pellets from a repeating rifle.

These were the qualities and weaknesses that early showed themselves in his parliamentary career; and one thing of which no-one would dream of accusing him was lack of energetic application to his work in the House. He was no part-time careerist; he virtually gave up paid employment as a lawyer to devote himself to public affairs; and this may well have been considered foolhardy—he had gained a seat in the House after a recount which showed him a victor by 18 votes. It was an extremely marginal constituency, and very soon after he had won it there was another general election in which he was victorious once more by a mere 196 votes. The future of his career hung on a decision by less than a hundred vacillating constituents.

A third election followed three or four years later, which showed that in spite of the impression he had made in the House, his majority remained precisely the same—less than two hundred votes. In these circumstances, he might easily have been forgiven if he had given some heed to an alternative occupation—a paid one. He was hardly to know that he would continue uninterrupted service in the House for some fifty years, that his majority henceforth would grow and grow until victory was automatic and his position unassailable, and his representation as Member for Caernarvon Boroughs an institution with almost as legendary a character as that of the Eisteddfod.

Great guts he always had; the reader will forgive the plainness of the description but I can think of no other that serves my meaning as well. He had little money—all his savings were spent—but he continued to turn down soft, safe sinecure jobs, supplementing a tiny income with kindred work as a political correspondent. There was the House and there was the Country, and he would take the consequences of service to them both.

A final remark about these marginal elections. Two of them had been fought against Squire Nanney, the Tory candidate. I knew Ellis Nanney quite well in the years that followed. He was a charming, kindly character, in spite of his bogy landlordism and Toryism; and we became quite good friends. He was most unremarkable, and history will always remember him for only one thing—that he opposed young Mr Lloyd George in two of his early elections; but there is a story which he told me that

70

certainly would deserve its place in a far better biography than this.

Nanney, in spite of his Toryism, was a very good landlord in some ways, and he had installed some excellent and what were then novel domestic facilities in some of the cottages on his land. During the final election contest with my father, he visited one of these cottages and expressed a mild interest to see one of these installations. He was taken to the small room in the house and shown the lavatory pan. It was as installed, but the lavatory seat, a handsome, mahogany, well-veneered and polished affair, was unaccountably missing. He turned to his host: 'Yes, that's right. I can see it's in good order. But tell me—what has happened to the nice mahogany seat?' 'Seat? You mean that round wooden frame?' 'Yes, that's right.' 'Oh, we've got Mr Lloyd George's face in it!' And there, in the parlour, Squire Nanney found the magnificently framed picture of his opponent.

I told the story to my father; and he roared.

9

MY earliest recollection of my father as a Member of
Parliament is a very hazy one. I *think* that what I thought
about the matter was that father worked in a House, a
sort of monster workshop for grown-ups, and attended by all
family providers, masculine variety. When the situation was clari-
fied, and I understood that this House was a rather privileged
institution, attended by an elect assembly, I took this in my stride,
too. My father was rather special, after all. I was fully prepared to
regard that fact with perfect equanimity. (My mother was even
more special—but I shall not inflict superlatives on the reader on
that subject.) My father in the House of Commons. Very praise-
worthy, but perfectly understandable; a natural phenomenon.
A more senior boy at school once buttonholed me amidst a group
of juniors. 'You Lloyd George?'
'Yes.'
'Your father David Lloyd George?'
'Yes.'
'Coo. Doesn't he *talk*!'
I think I blushed, partly with embarrassment and partly with
pride for having attracted the attention of a senior boy. And it
seemed that my small junior friends looked at me with a certain
curiosity, even vague interest—then they returned to the more
important business of marbles or whatever we were playing at the
time, and everything was as before.
I don't think that in the early years of my schooldays anyone
bothered very much with my father's political activities. I was
asked once or twice, in a friendly way, about whether I'd ever
met Mr Gladstone or somebody equally eminent; and I roundly
declared that he was due to have tea with us on Sunday. But these
were isolated moments of limelight, mildly welcomed and rather
amusing if not a little embarrassing, in the even tenor of school-

boy casualness. For the main part I was Dick, the little Welsh boy, myself, *me*, a well-rounded small personality with a coterie of special friends, a fair hand with a catapult, and far more famous for my possession of a genuine shell-handled clasp-knife than my political antecedent.

One day, when I went to school, I felt a violent blow in the small of my back. I gasped and turned in dismay to face one of the older school bullies. 'Dirty pro-Boer! Yah!'

In the weeks that followed my father's political personality became an absolute nightmare figure that haunted me every moment I was at school. I understood little or nothing of what the aggressiveness was all about; all I knew was that I had become a sort of whipping-boy for my father's political crimes. There was a kind of hysteria. Small boys as well as large ones—children I had hardly exchanged a word with in the past—baited me, abused me or pursued me remorselessly to kick me in the bony places—boys have an instinctive anatomical knowledge about the more vulnerable places.

At first I was bewildered and more aggrieved by my friends' 'denunciations' than by their physical attacks. I suppose I should have told my parents about what was going on, but youngsters have their own secret inhibitions and schoolboys their curious codes of loyalty. I felt that there must be a profound misunderstanding somewhere, but this really had nothing to do with my parents or masters, that it was between me and my fellows at school.

But I was semi-articulate; I could not reason. I did not know how to assemble the arguments. I could not put forward my case—look, chaps, this is me, Dick. Dick Wales. You know. What's wrong with you fellows? I'm just the same as I ever was. My father's all right. I don't understand much about what he's doing, but it must be all right; he must have his reason.

The words just would not come out.

Neither did I appeal to my father.

I heard my parents discuss the problem or the trouble in very guarded terms during my presence, so I suspected that father, too, had his share of it. But he did not look to me unduly concerned; he never seemed to worry very much—never at any time mentioned it—and neither did mother. I thought they were very brave indeed, both of them. I had always known this, and I thought it was up to me to solve my problem myself.

The little I understood about what was going on suggested to me that father was standing up for the little fellow, as he had done over Wales. I got that idea somehow into my head, and it stuck. Well, I suppose I was the little fellow at school, too, so I knew just how it felt, and how important that someone should stick up for him.

Those were days of great fear—and vast, vague pride—a pride reinforced by my mother's serene and cheerful strength. They were days of wonderful affection between my parents, and it radiated to us, the children; and there we were, in our little Welsh fortress, secure and strong, in the midst of danger. I took this certain emotional cue from my mother, my barometer, that if there was anything *wrong* about father, she would have indicated it to me by her attitude. She didn't, therefore they were all wrong—all of them outside at school, *and father was all right.*

So I continued my silence.

In the end, after several weeks of bullying, baiting, ostracism—I could no longer disguise my misery. Mother questioned me and I told her. Without hesitation, my parents arranged for me to go to a school in Merioneth. A terrible experience was at an end.

Of course, the facts about the Boer War are well known, and as this does not pretend to be a history of Lloyd George's times, I would only remind readers very briefly about them. The Boers originally were Dutch settlers driven by the encroaching British to make a great trek across the Drakensberg Mountains and form separate colonies. Conflict with the Bantu tribes made the British extend their frontiers close to the borders of these colonies, as African distances go, which led to the discovery of diamond mines near Kimberley. This of course attracted the British and other contingents of prospectors. There was trouble with the Boers; and then, with the discovery of great gold deposits on the Rand in the Transvaal, the foreign invasions of prospectors and diggers, British and European, grew to such an enormous scale that they outnumbered the Dutch citizenry by about four to one in their own territory.

It became an impossible situation in its anomaly—the prospectors and foreign workers demanded enfranchisement (they paid 95 per cent of the taxes for the whole Boer territory). Kruger, their president, equivocated. London sounded war alarums. There were sword clanking and troop movements on the British side. And the Boers took the daring course of trying to nip the threatened campaign against them in the bud. Their commandos struck.

It was a desperate policy, and their leaders thought that they would in time gain European allies. Thus began a war which dragged on for years.

There was a lot of political 'double think' at home—after all, it was the Boers who started the fighting, it was argued; but Lloyd George refused to have his judgment clouded by false reasoning and jingoist fervour. To him the issues were plain; there were three—pounds, shillings and pence.

He rose to speak in the House on an evening in February (1900). He made the finest, most closely-reasoned, scathing, forceful and courageous speech that had been heard in the House within the memory of its audience.

He reminded the House that the government had been warned by the former Commander-in-Chief at the Cape that the movement of troops to the Transvaal border would be a threatening act which the Boers could not ignore. He told them that more than fifty thousand soldiers would be needed from Britain to fight the coming war. The claim that the British government could 'run' the Transvaal better than its present rulers was arrogant, hypocritical and fatuous—the wages of the miners in the Transvaal was four times that of miners in Britain, and they had an eight-hour day; the Transvaal charged the mine owners fifty per cent royalties as against one-half per cent in Britain. The prospectors and foreign mine owners demanded British rule in order to be able to enforce their workers to accept smaller wages and longer hours on the British pattern. 'Look—here is the key to the whole picture—L. S. D.!' The very men who most strongly supported a franchise for the newcomers to the territory, and would have persuaded Kruger to accept this policy, had been forced by the British troop movements to lead the Commandos in their campaign to forestall a British invasion. And what of the Uitlanders (the prospectors) for whose 'rights' soldiers from Britain were to be sent six thousand miles? They were lounging in the bars of the comfortable hotels—they had mustered barely a battalion of troops. Was it worth shedding a drop of British blood for such men?

Such were some of the incisive points which earned Lloyd George the resentment, the fury, the antagonism and the admiration of the Members. They hated his speech, but they paid it tribute. Balfour said that he disagreed with every word, but thought it the most brilliant speech he had ever heard in the House. With the eccentric genius for sportsmanship which characterises certain products of the English public schools, they paid him compliments or passed him notes of congratulations, wishing him in hell, of course, at the same time.

The speech hurt—it was intended to; and when Lloyd George took it to the country in a whirlwind campaign, there were no compliments to temper the fury it roused. There was a violent aggressive feeling which would not be sated with anything except a nice blood-bath. It always strikes me as a curious aspect of human nature, this love of aggression. After all, my father was only trying to prevent Englishmen from shedding their blood in a piece of senseless butchery some six thousand miles from their homes and places of business; but they were determined to go or to send their brothers, their sons, their friends to fight in a war for a gang of cosmopolitan adventurers and opportunists who themselves kept pretty clear of gunshot.

Lloyd George was a most combative advocate for his pacifism, however, and I think it was probably the manner of his opposition as much as its subject matter which thoroughly roused the crowds he addressed. For one thing, he never minced any words about personalities. He made his special target Joseph Chamberlain, the Colonial Secretary, who had the misfortune to be associated with a family business that manufactured armaments. Joe Chamberlain had been a very formidable personality in his time, with an attacking technique that terrified his opponents; but like the Bishop of St Asaph, he met his match in Lloyd George. The contests between them had the character of engagements between a young panther and a proud bull buffalo a little past his fighting days who had felt himself entitled to an honourable retirement from the arena. Lloyd George's lightning assaults—short, rending attacks and clean breakaways—left the old warrior dazed, hurt and almost inarticulate. His usual retort was in the 'Who—me?' category; and God help him if he tried to counter-attack.

The conduct of the war—the extraordinary blunders in the early part of the campaign which almost lost the jingoists South Africa altogether to the Boers—presented fine targets to Lloyd George, who had ample opportunities to make use of the full range of his armoury, including the acid of derision. And there were the diplomatic blunders—the failure to make an honourable peace when the opportunity was clearly there; the strategic blunders later in the campaign, when a small band of mobile Commandos, fighting in the extra dimension of movement, played havoc with the static block-house defence of the British forces; and the humane blunders, the concentration camps for the Boer women and children, where conditions were so wretched that at the close of hostilities it was estimated that twice as many women and children died during the campaign as Boer troops. Needless to say, Lloyd George did not miss a point. His tireless, dangerous, bitter crusade made him outstandingly the greatest personality of his day, and the most notorious.

He took his life in his hands every time he mounted a public platform. He made trips to all the tough trouble spots. In his own constituency he was almost killed one night in the street—coshed over the head, knocked senseless and saved from being trampled in the crowd by the courage of a small band of friends and the police.

During the Khaki Election fought in the middle of the war, he achieved an almost unique triumph in turning popular feeling against him. He seemed certain to lose his parliamentary seat, but the crucial speech he made to save his career had so much moral force that the belligerent, antagonistic crowd that came to abuse and volley missiles was first silenced, and then was moved to demonstrate wildly in his favour. It was a remarkable feat of oratory. I think this passage from his speech is the noblest of his career: 'Five years ago, the electors of the Caernarvon Boroughs gave to me my strip of blue paper, the certificate of my election, to hand to the Speaker of Parliament as your accredited representative. If I never again represent the Caernarvon Boroughs in the House of Commons, I shall at least have the satisfaction of handing back to you that blue paper with no stain of human blood upon it.'

The emotional appeal was successful when all the logic in the world would have failed; and this was an aspect of human psychology that my father had observed particularly strongly during his anti-war campaign. In one of the more intimate, rather special moments, he once told me that emotional temperature always ruled the main points of argument. Here he was fighting as an irregular, a rebel against authority or what today is known as the Establishment. That was his nature; all his politics had sprung from that state of feeling, and the arguments he used selected themselves to fit the pattern of his feelings. He was emotionally drawn to the side of the 'little fellow'—in later years his war convictions were framed only from the time of the invasion of Belgium, the 'little fellow' again; and this time, too, he could identify the struggle according to the lights of his own nature. The public school representatives in the House could not accept his arguments, or even understand them, because they instinctively marched with the big battalions. 'A brilliant speech, Lloyd George! I hated every word of it.' In his more disillusioned moments he sometimes wondered whether rational arguments ever really had an effect on serious, fundamental questions. Conservatism and Radicalism were peculiarities of one's nature, like the pigmentation of the skin, he once said to me.

The mass of the people were not emotionally committed in the way the die-hards were in the House; and he knew that his only chance to bring the useless war to a close was to go to the people, appeal to them, coax them, insult them, deride them, bully them into an understanding of what these issues really were and what they meant to the common man. In his own constituency, at least, he succeeded. He risked death; and he saved his career.

There were, of course, other 'irregulars', other British commandos—Keir Hardie, a newcomer to the House; and the Liberal

Party was split on the war question. Few of his progressive colleagues took his dangerous course. The questions were argued in the banqueting rooms of fashionable restaurants—'war to the knife-and-fork', as he grimly quoted.

The climax of his campaign took place in Birmingham, but before dealing with it, it is interesting to note that he formed an important friendship at the time, which was to last some forty years, with a new member in the House, a former officer in the African war.

This former soldier said in the House, 'The situation is disquieting, and the position as momentous as it was two years ago before the first shot was fired'.

Lloyd George quoted him with enthusiasm when answering the charge that his own words were giving comfort and support to the Boers. 'Why, look what Mr Churchill says! Now, we know him! This is that young fellow we caught on the armoured train, a bright, intelligent young lad he is! And he is going around Britain declaring that for the British the situation is becoming disquieting. Well, this is most encouraging!'

The two young men had looked at each other across the House, and although they were on opposite Benches, they had recognised each other as kindred spirits. Although a Tory, young Mr Churchill was as fearless in criticising his own leaders as he was many years later in opposition before the Hitler war—and for the same sort of bungling, muddling, nepotistic conduct of affairs involving life and death for their countrymen.

The Birmingham Peace Meeting was the most riotous of the 'Lloyd George Nights'. Birmingham was the Joe Chamberlain political stronghold. The Chamberlains—Joe, Austen and later Neville—had a grip there which went far beyond political sympathy. The Chamberlains were the local royal family, and seemed to enact a self-designated rôle which combined authority, patronage and devotion to their populace. Joe was the first and the greatest of the Chamberlain father figures.

Lloyd George's baiting and snapping and worrying of their popular hero had a far greater effect on the temper of the Birmingham motley even than his 'pro-Boer' campaign; and the two combined drove them to a happy frenzy of aggressiveness. Both the Birmingham Liberal Association and the local Chief Constable wrote to warn Lloyd George that he would be taking his life in his hands to hold a peace meeting there, so he promptly set a date and started packing his bags.

The Birmingham Press welcomed their distinguished guest by explaining carefully that a few years ago he would have been hanged as a traitor. They obligingly published his picture prominently in their journals.

His 'reception committee' outside the Town Hall, where the meeting was to be held, were armed with bottles containing chemicals, bricks and other sundry weapons. They massed in their thousands to trample him into the ground, conscious that in anonymity murder would escape individual retribution.

The problem that confronted his friends was first to get him into the Town Hall, alive. All sorts of plans were proposed to ensure his safe arrival on the platform. Strong-arm squads of stewards, flanked by police and preceded by *cavalry* was suggested.

'Not a single bodyguard. Not a policeman—not a soldier, mounted or otherwise,' said Lloyd George.

He proposed simply that the only 'safe' method to secure passage through the crowd would be if he went and mingled with the 'reception committee' alone. They would be on the lookout for an escort, he explained with a simple air of reason.

When his friends recovered from their shock at such almost insensate boldness, they tried desperately to dissuade him from this course; but he was adamant. He refused to provoke a pitched battle between the local population and the military in his behalf.

'Well, at any rate, you must disguise yourself completely,' his fearfully anxious friends pleaded.

Lloyd George did not regard this as very practical. 'If I start putting on greasepaint and funny hats, I would be singled out. Better go as I am,' he said.

His only disguise was to put on a different overcoat and a peaked cap. He drove to Victoria Square in a carriage, and there alighted and strolled casually through the marauding crowds of demonstrators, by imperceptible stages drawing closer and closer to the entrance of the Hall.

Amidst the chanting and shouting and yelling of the frenzied thousands who alternated proclamations of their devotion to Soldiers of the Queen, the 'Boys at the Front' with bloodthirsty exhortations to do violence to 'Krujer' and the dirty traitor, Lloyd George, he was a sublimely detached and lonely figure,

It was more than a hundred paces through that mob and every step was as dangerous as the precipitous ascent of a rocky pinnacle. One false move, one more than casual glance at him, one accidental shove that unsettled his cap, would have proved fatal. Hesitation, sudden alarm, a hurrying stride, any outward suggestion of his fear would have drawn attention to himself.

Once inside, there was no escape in the ordinary way. When the crowds realised that he was in the Hall, pandemonium started. They tore down barricades, made a battering ram and forced the doors of the entrance, breaking through the cordons of stewards and police like a tidal wave. Seven thousand people were jammed in the Hall, a large proportion of them struggling with the defenders of the would-be speaker.

Lloyd George, unable to make himself heard, calmly dictated his 'speech' on the platform to a secretary and one or two local reporters, whilst the outcome of the battle between his defenders (reinforced by the police) and the mob was decided. Having completed dictating his speech he allowed himself to be barricaded in one of the Committee Rooms, where the Chief Constable tried to persuade him to put on a police uniform and seek safety in this disguise. The attackers were constantly being reinforced by the mob outside and to prevent further injury and destruction Lloyd George reluctantly agreed to conceal his identity in this 'somewhat undignified' fashion; and he was able to find safety eventually, mingling with the police and slipping through the rioters in the disguise of a police constable. Even then there was a nasty moment when one of the crowd recognised him; but his rioting pals made so much noise that the triumphant eureka cries could not be heard.

The Brummagem riot resulted in a death and a large number of injuries—forty people being detained in hospital. The mob burst into every room in the Town Hall, destroying everything they could lay their hands on in their fury of frustration. Amongst the items of damage were slightly more than a thousand broken windows.

And before his next meeting in Bristol, a telegram was sent to him from his pro-Chamberlain well-wishers—'That Bristol will go one better than we did and crack your skull in is the sincere wish of all Birmingham'.

STATESMAN

I

THE period shortly after the Boer War showed a maturing of Lloyd George's powers as parliamentarian. There were two issues, important at the time (although now they seem rather academic in interest)—the Education Act, the practical effect of which (from Lloyd George's point of view) would be to increase the influence of English Church instruction in the Nonconformist school communities, and the attempt to introduce Imperial Preference. Lloyd George was a great Free Trader.

In the debates that followed on these questions, Lloyd George showed himself more than ever before master of his material.

The *Daily News* wrote: 'Until Lloyd George spoke tonight, Nonconformity, its intellectual attitude to Education, its historical associations with the settlement of 1870, now being torn up, and its contribution to the religious problem, had gone without a recorder and a champion. Mr Lloyd George took that vacant place tonight.'

The other issue—that some preference be shown to importers of wheat from the Empire—started a controversy in the House that was to last some twenty-five years between the Tariff Reformers and Free Traders. It was a fire which was never completely quenched in this period except during the war years. When we think of the economic issues today, with arguments for the communal ownership of vast industries embodied in the policy of a major political party, these old disputes seem to have a storm-in-the-teacup air about them; in fact, the first dispute that provoked that marathon contest, whether the principle (free trade) could be abandoned, in practical terms meant an increase of less than half a farthing on a fourpenny loaf.

The whole issue is equivocal—whether it is better to safeguard the interests of the community by having goods at the cheapest world competitive prices, or whether these safeguards are more effective if the industries themselves are protected, thus ensuring full employment, cannot really involve 'principle'; and the ethical significance of the contest featured more in the minds of the debaters than in reality. The community as a whole regarded the argument as an academic one. In an age of ferocious industrial upheaval, with huge ugly sores on the body politic—poverty, prostitution, crime, disease, deeply entrenched privilege, sombre manœuvring in the sphere of world power politics—such technical matters were more properly the business of a committee of economists; and my father, referring to this period some time later, told me, in a moment of gloom, that he wished Parliament had been free then to debate the great social and economic issues of poverty, unemployment and inherited economic privilege, so as to anticipate problems which arose in all their aggravated form during the dithering 'twenties and hungry 'thirties.

I remember a wonderful little passage of arms between my father and H. G. Wells at home, with the great novelist and sociologist baiting L. G. over what he called the 'patchwork' economic policy of those former times—'cutting a piece of the tail of the shirt to mend the hole in the collar'. H. G. was an excitable debater, and his thin pugnacious voice rose to a squeak of triumph as he out-Lloyded George in his own method of argument. I think that on this occasion, at any rate, he won hands down.

But it was a fruitful period of inexorable progress for the still (politically) young man. He was now outstandingly the most talented and formidable of the 'new men', and destined for high office in the natural course of events. His chance came with Balfour's resignation in 1905 and the formation of a new government under Campbell-Bannerman.

I think he had a 'feeling' about this turning point in his career. He sometimes suffered from a malady of the throat. Now (I think) there was nothing wrong with his throat. It troubled him when he was in a nervous state—a mental state—on the eve of a particularly important debate, sometimes. His throat was the channel of expression of his political personality. Sometimes it distressed him, as if shutting up shop to give him his excuse to plead incapacity through force of circumstances in some critical testing period. The doctors did not understand this aspect of him, and when he complained of pains in this area of the vocal organs they accepted his complaints literally, diagnosed tonsillitis and operated. It nearly cost him his life. Sitting at home shortly after the operation, his throat suddenly began to bleed profusely. A Welsh specialist was hastily summoned; and had he been delayed a few minutes my father would have died.

This throat 'complaint', coming on the eve of his appointment as President of the Board of Trade, was no coincidence, in my view. He knew that a testing period of magnitude awaited him; and it 'went to this throat' in much the same way as it affected his knee joints in the incident previously described when he was faced with the simple (but for him, highly nostalgic and emotional) task of paying tribute to the late King of the Belgians.

He went to convalesce in Italy, and whilst there received a coded message from Uncle William about important political changes. He hurried home, to find himself a Cabinet Minister in the new government.

He was in fine company in his new office—Asquith (future Prime Minister), Chancellor of the Exchequer; Grey, Foreign Minister; Churchill (future Prime Minister and war leader), Under-Secretary for the Colonies. (Churchill had crossed the floor of the House to join 'the best fighting general in the Liberal Party, Lloyd George'.) Campbell-Bannerman led a Cabinet which, as history would know, contained three future Prime Ministers amongst his colleagues.

Lloyd George, as President of the Board of Trade, had the most complex technical administration task: shipping, land transport, the electricity council, industrial patents, bankruptcy and company law. He entered on his work with a sense of diffidence—he had no expert knowledge of any of these matters, and at first felt unhappily at a disadvantage. He quickly realised that it would have been impossible for any one person to embrace a professional knowledge of every department, and the deference yielded to an exciting new sense of opportunity. It was expected that the Minister would allow the departments to carry on with permanent Civil Servants, and not 'interfere' in any matters of deep-established policy. He might re-shuffle a few heads of departments or bring some promising newcomer forward—and then let them carry on. Changes would 'accrue' by this tried old method, the departments carrying on in their comfortable inertia, stimulated into a few minor changes by a short-lived game of departmental musical chairs. In the House, his experts would give him material necessary to answer parliamentary questions. (How else could a Minister manage in such circumstances? An expert on company law, a Minister might be—he could not be an expert on the electricity council as well, and combine with that a working knowledge of shipping, and so on.)

Lloyd George did something unprecedented. He took each department in turn, and thoroughly grounded himself in a general knowledge of its ways. The departmental heads soon found that he was able to talk about matters that concerned them on their level. But there the affinity ended. The permanent officials had the usual limitation of outlook which preferred a comfortable routine to disturbing radical change, even if it were probably for the better. They did not reckon with the temperament of their new chief. Lloyd George was not content to know that such and such was so. He wanted to know why it was like that, whether someone had ever suggested an alternative; what that alternative was; and why it hadn't been tried out if it hadn't been tried out.

He would get together all the experts of the department and take the chair at meetings in which everything was thrown into the melting pot in discussion, nothing taken for granted. He provoked, stimulated, invited ideas, suggestions. And all the time his own ranging imagination was at work in committee. It was a wonderful example of dynamic imagination at work—not imagination in the poetic sense: his was the sort that operated in practical matters. He liked *doing* things. He liked getting *things done*.

His colleagues were astonished when the Board of Trade, that primmest and starchiest of all departments, some of whose offices had not known a change for nearly fifty years, began to hum with life. The House was more than impressed by the way the new Minister tackled his department. It is the time-honoured privilege of Opposition members to provide the stimulus for departmental change. In the case of the Board of Trade, the members had the sensation of trying to pick up a suitcase they thought was full, and being completely thrown off balance when it suddenly flew into their faces, weightless . . . a most peculiar sensation.

It is generally accepted that in his term of office at the Board of Trade, Lloyd George effected more progressive change than in the ministry's entire history, and laid the foundations of the modern Board. He codified the shipping laws (Merchant Shipping Act of 1906)—a very technical and complex problem in that transitional period from sail to steam; he hammered out a more satisfactory formula for patents' registration, which protected British rights abroad; a new Companies Act, which ensured protection for shareholders and creditors; an international agreement for the Consular service; a Census of Production Act. Among the more important statutes was a safeguard to workers, compensation for injuries in the course of employment; and there was the famous Seamen's Charter.

And he weeded out the fuddy-duddies.

He told me how he had occasion to consult the head of the Electricity Board. He summoned the gentleman, a rather benign elderly party, who was very ill at ease to be interrogated about his department. 'I'll have to consult Mr So and So,' he said after a while. L. G. waited. The elderly gentleman shuffled and looked embarrassed. 'Well?' L. G. prompted. The elderly gentleman pointed to the rather weird, prehistoric intercom appliance on L. G.'s desk. 'How do you work this?' the head of the Electricity Board asked the Minister.

With this experience of committee work, Lloyd George grew very confident in his rôle as negotiator. He vastly enjoyed—at any time—exercising the power of his personality; and when an industrial crisis arose which embarrassed the government, he offered his services as mediator. Campbell-Bannerman was relieved to let the young enthusiast try his hand. Arbitrating in industrial disputes is a delicate and difficult business, and fear of failure (which would have thrown discredit on the conciliator) often paralyses the hand of authority. It was remarkable that with an old, experienced Labour man in the Cabinet, John Burns (hero

89

of the famous dock strike in the 'eighties), the P.M. preferred to entrust the business to the President of the Board of Trade. No doubt, he thought that the author of the Seamen's Charter and the Workmen's Compensation Act would have the sympathies of Labour; and anyone who could navigate the subtle reefs of the shipping code would find his way safely to harbour in the cross-currents between employers and workmen.

In this extra-curricular task, Lloyd George also proved successful. The Government were relieved; the P.M. was delighted. Campbell-Bannerman's 'new boy' was beginning to beat a path to the highest office.

Sir Henry Campbell-Bannerman was a sick man, and for a long time doctors had urged him to relieve himself of the most responsible office in the country. In 1908 he retired from politics altogether; Asquith became Prime Minister. The Chancellorship, vacated by this change, was given to Lloyd George.

At the age of forty-five, Lloyd George moved into the post traditionally second in importance only to that of the Prime Minister; and he took up residence at No. 11, Downing Street, with the Premier his next-door neighbour.

On the evening in April that he went to Buckingham Palace to see the King, he should have been one of the happiest men in England. It rained that day and when he came home his cheeks were wet. We thought it was the rain; but my mother asked him tenderly why he had wept, and she kissed him.

'I cried because I knew my little Mair would not be at home to share my happiness.'

My sister Mair, his best-beloved child, had recently died from an attack of appendicitis.

2

OUR family.
     At first we were three. Father, mother and I. Then
followed Mair, Olwen and Gwilym in that order. They
joined us, it seemed to me in my childhood days, in rather an
arbitrary fashion. I was told calmly and casually about each new
arrival in what I felt was a typically high-handed grown-up
manner. Nobody ever consulted me!

'You have a new brother,' I was told one day as I returned
home from school. I felt considerably put out. I had no opportunity to examine his qualifications, his worthiness in becoming a
member of our very select club. I was assured that everything was
in order, although I formed no high opinion of Gwilym when
originally introduced to him.

I had the satisfaction of being the eldest of the children, whom
the rest had to treat with proper respect. It may be interesting to
English readers to know that in our family a certain protocol was
punctiliously observed. There was, for instance, a different form
of address between the junior and senior members of the family.
The elders were 'chi', the equivalent of the formal and respectful
'you'. Juniors were 'chdi', the intimate and familiar 'thee'. (There
are equivalents in other languages, of course; the French 'vous'
and 'tu'; the German 'du' and 'sie', and so on.) I was 'chi' to all
the other children; and to me they were all 'chdi'. Mair 'chi'd'
me and 'chdi'd' the others. Olwen addressed me and Mair as
'chi', was 'chdi' to us and respectfully 'chi'd' by Gwilym. Gwilym
had to mind his 'chis' and was 'chdi' to all of us.

We were a pretty combustible mixture of our parents' volatile
and serene temperaments. Olwen, Gwilym and I were a bit of
a handful, normally mischievous. Olwen was magnificently
formidable when roused; Gwilym slow to anger and then a real
Lloyd George when driven beyond his small, patient endurance.

Mair alone was sweetness and light. She had one of those wonderful, angelic dispositions, a remarkable sensitivity and early maturity, which is the pride of parents and envious admiration of other children. She was spared nothing in the way of looks and talent—a beautiful girl and always top of her class at school. Megan, who came a good deal later, was the Personality; bright, forthright and yet subtle, with a drive and energy that compensated fully for her minuteness—but then dynamite comes in small packages.

Olwen was later to go to school at Roedean, completing her education in Dresden. She formed a very happy marriage with Sir Thomas Carey Evans, a brilliant surgeon, and had four children. On balance, I think that she has more brains than the rest of the Lloyd George offsprings in our family, combining wisdom with her inherited wit.

Gwilym and Megan, of course, had parliamentary careers. Gwilym followed father's footsteps and achieved ministerial rank. He was one of the most popular ministers in the House in his time, but I feel he erred most unhappily when he was Home Secretary over the Ruth Ellis tragedy. He should never have allowed that mentally-disturbed, passionate young woman to hang for a crime committed in a moment's aberration of feminine jealousy.

Megan had real parliamentary gifts. It is nearly always a help to have an influential parent in one's chosen career; but sometimes it is a disadvantage. I think that in Megan's case, father's influence was more a handicap than a support—he was such a strong personality that she suffered all her life both from his direct dominance and the knowledge that she had to compete with the dazzling radiance of his pre-eminent position in world politics.

I had decided to become an engineer; I qualified at Cambridge, and did my best, allowing for the interruption of two world wars, to make a career for myself in the 'twenties and 'thirties at a time of mass unemployment which deeply affected our profession.

The Lloyd Georges in residence at Downing Street, with their Welsh servants, must have presented a weird spectacle to their English friends and visitors—the wild clansmen from foreign parts picnicking in the heart of Westminster. I sympathise with Sir Arthur Salter when he relates one of these experiences.

'A critical question arose at the week-end in connection with the National Health Insurance Commission (with which I was working at the time), which required urgent ministerial decision. Two other officials and myself went to see C. F. G. Masterman, the Minister directly concerned, on the Sunday afternoon. He decided that Lloyd George himself must be consulted, and we all went round to 11, Downing Street, to tea, Rufus Isaacs (Lord Reading) being at some stage added to the party. When we arrived we found Lloyd George, with Mrs Lloyd George and other members of his family, standing round the piano singing hymns with great gusto. We were all swept in, making, I fear, a rather incongruous chorus for such an occupation.

'I recall breakfasting with him (L. G.), Mrs Lloyd George and one or two members of the family. He was in his best form, as he was usually from the moment he woke—most men prefer a solitary or silent breakfast and take time to warm up like a cold engine, but he never. He convulsed us all with one tale after another. When he paused for a moment, Mrs Lloyd George, with tears running down her face with laughter, turned to me and said, "You wouldn't think I should laugh so at his jokes after all these years, would you? But I can't help it." It made a conversation piece of a peculiarly pleasing domestic scene.'

My father's prowess as a raconteur was of such a nature that I would listen avidly even when I knew the story (or thought I knew it)—for he would unashamedly embellish it according to the fancy of the moment, like all really skilled story-tellers, mixing fancy with fact to heighten effect.

He related, for instance, when as Chancellor of the Exchequer he had to go up to town for a reception at the Guildhall. We had taken a house at Walton Heath at the time, which mother preferred to the official residence, and he travelled in our vintage Napier. The reception was an Affair, and father was resplendently attired in regalia—knee breeches, long stockings, silverbuckled pumps, sword and cloak. Our car was not fitted with electricity in those distant days, the headlights being acetylene. On the journey home from the reception the headlights failed. It was a moonless and very dark night, so the chauffeur got out and started to examine the cause of the trouble. After a while, my father became impatient, left the car and walked off down the lonely country road ahead of it, expecting to be picked up in due course.

A few minutes later, father heard the car coming and waved to notify the chauffeur of his presence. The chauffeur, however, had not noticed that father had left his car and roared past him with olympian aloofness, refusing to add a hitch-hiker to the Chancellor's equipage.

There was father, in his cloak, sword and silver-buckled pumps in the middle of a country lane at night, stranded. Swearing vehemently, he proceeded on his way.

Now this was one version, comical enough—the Chancellor of the Exchequer in knee breeches and plumed hat trying to cadge a lift as a hitch-hiker. But being father, the story would not end there. He gave it many variedly climactic endings. One of these—his favourite—was that after a long and exhausting trek, he found himself at the gates of a large mansion. He groped his way inside and approached a large, formidable entrance. He hammered on it for a long time. At last he heard massive locks turned and the door opened. An official-looking, grim figure stood truculently in the doorway.

'I'm sorry to disturb you. My car broke down and I was left stranded. May I come in? I am the Chancellor of the Exchequer.'

'Certainly. Do come in. The rest of the Cabinet have been expecting you.'

Now there *was* a lunatic asylum in the neighbourhood, and the story might have been true; but knowing father, I am sure that this charming *dénouement* was a fantasy with which the old man regaled himself when he was making his way home to lighten the tedium of the journey.

Such were the stories related in company when visitors were present; for the family occasion, the anecdotes had a much saltier flavour. Remembering my parents' background, it will probably surprise no one that they fluently related rather earthy stories, and these often were combined with a religious background, a contrast that gave them piquancy.

Here are two of my favourites.

A famous Welsh preacher and a very close friend of L. G., Dr Charles Williams of Menai Bridge, received a deputation of deacons who wanted to excommunicate one of their colleagues. The offender had married a woman, and the next day he left her and refused henceforth to live with her.

'Why such fickleness?' asked Dr Williams.

'He discovered on their wedding night that his wife had a wooden leg,' the spokesman of the deputation said. (It will be appreciated that these were Victorian days when ladies wore skirts that covered their unmentionables.)

'No, I shall not advise his excommunication,' Dr Williams said. 'He has obviously proved himself to be an exceptionally virtuous man. Not one of you would not have found it out beforehand.'

One of the most famous of Welsh preachers, the Reverend Evan Jones, had occasion to reprimand an erring member of his flock, a young girl who had sinned wantonly.

Arrived at her home, he tried to put her at her ease. 'Well, now, Mary *bach*, tell me what happened.'

"Well, Mr Jones, sir, he asked me to go for a walk in the wood with him and I went one evening. We walked for a while and as it was very fine he said we should sit down. We sat down and talked, and after a while he became very loving, and fondled me and started to kiss me—Oh, Mr Jones, sir, he started to kiss me something fierce, and I was quite breathless—and I fainted. And I don't remember any more.'

'*Wel Mari Bach, mi gollaist y sport igyd!*' said old Evan. ('Mary *bach*, but you missed all the fun!')

Now the reader will note that these stories concern clergymen whom my father knew, but whether they really happened, as he said to friends of his, or whether this was a story-teller's 'improvement' it is impossible to say.

I think that my favourite story with 'variations' or possible 'improvements' concerns my father's interest in phrenology. He was a life-long believer that the shape of men's heads, or their size, indicated their mental capacity. (He was a believer in graphology, too.) A rational man about most things, he was quite fanatical in his faith in the merits of these somewhat suspect 'sciences'.

His main tenet in phrenology was that the largeness of your head was in due proportion to your brain development, whatever that meant; and the only exception to this rule concerned Bonar Law, whose mental processes L. G. admired regardless. He sometimes enquired about the size hat a friend or visitor wore, with a casual air of unconcern, but I am sure that if this was unusually large he would immediately revise his opinion about its wearer.

He told me that one day he had an argument with a rather pompous financial magnate about this theory. The tycoon had left his hat on a chair in father's office, and whilst immersed in some documents and notes, did not observe L. G. remove it. Father folded some paper and slipped it inside the inner flap of the hat. After their business was concluded, father took the business man out to the front door and waited eagerly for him to put on his hat.

'Good-bye, Mr Lloyd George. I hope the matter will prove acceptable to you.' They shook hands and the tycoon put on his hat. He removed it and put it on once more. 'Odd. Very odd. My hat suddenly feels tight.'

'You see,' father said in triumph, 'one conversation with me——' And he made one of his eloquent gestures.

The visitor left hurriedly, looking back over his shoulder at the Welsh Wizard with consternation in his gaze.

With Sir James Barrie as an old family friend, no one need be surprised that both my parents indulged in fantasy spinning of the happiest kind. When father relaxed, it was complete gaiety and charming nonsense, like an excerpt from *Alice*, only rather more Rabelaisian.

Sitting in the sun-parlour at Brynawelon one clear, lovely day, mother suddenly sat up and said, 'Goodness! I can see St David's Head!'

As this promontory of Wales is about eighty miles distant from where they sat, father immediately responded to the challenge. He went into the house and brought out a pair of binoculars. 'You're right. St David's Head it is,' he said, peering through the lenses. 'There's Gwilym on the side of the hill.'

(*Above*) My father leaving Downing Street with Lord Birkenhead and Mr Churchill. This photograph must have been taken about 1920.

(*Below*) Addressing a crowd at Lampeter Station, 1919.

Electioneering: my father speaking during an election meeting at Camberwell in 1924 (*above*), and talking to voters on their own ground during a by-election (March 1929).

He lowered the binoculars.

Mother shaded her eyes. 'Gwilym? Oh, yes. How foolish of me not to notice.'

'Maggie,' he said with a serious air, 'you must talk to Gwilym about his absent-mindedness. One of his fly-buttons is unfastened.'

There was the incident of the fish. Father and I were both quite keen fishermen. I brought home a rather minute catch of trout, which were belittled by being served on the largest yeoman platter in the household. But I had the last laugh over this. Father brought home a catch of mackerel, which he insisted had to be specially cured. He proceeded to split and salt them; and then I found him solemnly hanging them up with clothes-pegs on the washing-line.

'What do you think this will do to them?' I dared to ask.

'Don't show your ignorance, my boy. They have to be exposed for thirty-six hours in the open. Then they will be fit for gourmets.'

The next morning only the bare heads of the fish remained pegged to the line. Our cats were most proficient high-jumpers.

I have mentioned some famous names as visitors and guests. For very many years a gossip columnist would have needed no other 'field research' than a standing invitation to the Lloyd Georges'. Artists, scientists, actors, great singers and executants, authors as well as politicians, frequently stayed with us. On the whole, they were far more interesting people than prominent socialites. I have mentioned Wells and Barrie. There were Irving, Beerbohm Tree, Melba, Patti, Dan Leno, Charlie Chaplin and many others who contributed to the fascinating gaiety of the social occasions. Sir Henry Irving and father discussing each other's 'stage' techniques was as nice a piece of shop talk as you're likely to come across. Irving thought father would have made a fine actor.

'*Would* have? I *am*.' 'Well, in that case, you're your own best playwright, too,' was the gracious tribute.

Sir James Barrie and father discussing a favourite topic—father was always interested in a play's 'message', if any. He wanted to know where Barrie 'stood' on a certain theme. In *Dear Brutus* Barrie had presented a theme that human beings are what they are irrespective of circumstances. 'The fault, dear Brutus, is not in our stars but in ourselves that we are underlings,' was quoted. 'But,' said father, 'in *The Admirable Crichton* you contend the very opposite. Given a classless environment, the natural leader emerges who is a butler in other circumstances.' (*Touché!*) We all looked at Barrie. He considered a moment. 'Well, Mr Churchill has crossed the floor of the House. What's good enough for Churchill——'

Possibly the only man who could have matched father in oratory during his prime was someone who never sat in the House of Commons in his entire career, the redoubtable Bernard Shaw; but there was one occasion when father silenced him absolutely and for ever in connection with one of his pet theories. Bernard Shaw would come down to breakfast to a special corner of the table which was cleared for him like a battlefield. He would practically barricade himself behind enormous boxes of brans, oats, corn flakes which he would mix with cream and butter-milk with the expertness of a cocktail steward.

Father said one morning, "Tell me, Shaw. Are you a vegetarian for health reasons or humane ones?"

'Both, certainly. Health reasons. I shall live to a hundred,' said the great individualist, with an aggressive tilt of his beard.

'Well,' father said, 'even if you don't, with that diet it will seem like that.' He added amiably, 'Humane reasons, too?'

'Of course. I eat nothing that has been killed.'

Father calmly put down his knife and fork. 'Do you eat cheese?'

'Of course.'

'But didn't you know that all cheese is made with the fluid of dairy animal pancreas?'

'What's that? I don't believe it!'

'My dear G. B. S., you must remember that I come from a farming community. A calf is always killed for the cheese making.'

The great man spluttered over his all-bran and pushed his plate away. For fifty years he had believed himself a complete vegetarian!

It was a little unkind, perhaps, but Shaw had behaved with

a great deal of arrogance, particularly to his wife, a very charming and intelligent woman.

There was a party of bigwigs on the lawn. Sir Hamar Greenwood, Winston Churchill, Lord Riddell, Eric Geddes and my father. All deep in conversation. Churchill was holding forth, waving his cigar. One of those vital if informal discussions in which big policies are thrashed out in the tranquillity of the great man's private occasion. What were they talking about? I hesitated to join them in case I would disturb some crucial argument that would determine the fate of nations.

Then my father turned to mother, who had just joined them. 'Maggie, would you please fetch a tape measure?'

'Yes, all right.'

Off she went, whilst my father and Eric Geddes stopped and carefully began to roll up their trouser legs. When she came back they asked her to measure their muscles. Geddes had boasted that his muscular development was three inches vaster than father's. Mother measured them each in turn and pronounced that Geddes' calf muscles were only half an inch broader than Lloyd George's. Father was pleased as punch. Winston's cigar wagged cockily. He had been the instigator of the contest!

Father was informally interviewing—this was a rare occasion— a Welsh journalist, who proved to be as opinionated as he was obtuse. Suddenly, in a flash of exasperation, father cut the discussion short. 'Well, there's one thing I can promise you, Mr Hugh Hughes. You'll never be in *Who's Who*,' he thundered, and stamped out into the garden.

3

THERE has been talk in recent years about personality cults. Now, of course, this is meat and drink to all experienced politicians. Winston, with his funny hats and his cigars, has been a boon to cartoonists. Lloyd George knew all about it long ago. His opera cloak and flowing mane were the theatrical props of his trade. One day he said at a public meeting that pheasants had ruined a field of mangold-wurzels on his farm. ('Now watch the fun,' father said to me later.) Sure enough the joke about Lloyd George's mangold-wurzels went the round of Fleet Street. Most newspapermen had to look up the word. They were firmly convinced that Lloyd George had invented the plant. When they discovered that in fact it did exist, they embraced their journalistic opportunities with rapture. Lloyd George and his mangold-wurzels became a national joke which endured throughout his entire career. A famous cartoonist unfailingly represented this plant in all his drawings of Lloyd George for about thirty years. L. G. was artful; the joke was really on Fleet Street.

In any case, Welsh people are like that. They exercise their tongues in their cheek more than most. For hundreds of years they have pretended that the leek is their national symbol, although this is a misconception due to the confusion of meanings attached to the word *cenin* (*Cenine Pedr*, the Welsh national symbol, means daffodil; but *cenin* is a leek). Through a translator's error, the English hilariously adopted the leek and the Welsh solemnly put a straight face on it, preferring the subtler fun of a secret joke at the expense of their English friends.

L. G. had the same sort of fun over his mangold-wurzels. And about his theatrical costume. And a dozen other things which provided publicity fun for millions of readers.

What was he really like as a personality? He had his eccentricities and unusual attributes. He had a remarkable ability to sleep at will, for instance. This was a source of strength to a man who sometimes had to work eighteen hours out of the twenty-four. An hour's nap between arduous conferences refreshed him, returning him to the contest with full energy. The habit proved a little disconcerting to his friends as well as his foes. There were times, in the middle of less formal meetings, when he would solemnly announce that he was tired and would now proceed to take a brief nap—which he did forthwith, sitting up at the conference table, for about ten minutes. Apart from the size of men's heads or their handwriting, he classified them by this Napoleonic trait, the sleepers and the non-sleepers.

His eating habits were a little extraordinary by orthodox standards; he enjoyed farinaceous and proteinous food (fried ham, beans and liver were favourites). He was a firm believer in the sustaining qualities of offal, kidneys, all the choice inner meats. He would say, 'The carnivorous animals always eat first the heart and liver of their prey. They know by instinct which are the most nutritious parts of the carcase'.

He greatly enjoyed, of course, mental excitement. But he adored physical excitement, too. He nearly got himself drowned in a small open boat which encountered a squall. The experience terrified him, but he enjoyed it so much that he insisted on taking command of a small yacht on a later occasion when a storm threatened, in spite of the entreaties of the captain and half the passengers and crew. I have described his love of storms, and his mounted ascent of the summits in the Andes. When he was in Naples one winter, he heard that Vesuvius was beginning to get lively again. Whilst almost all his friends hurriedly made off to catch a train, he insisted on climbing up to the crater, which was rumbling loudly, belching black sulphur-laden clouds and emitting tongues of flame. He stood defiantly on the rim of the giant cauldron, singing heartily. (His friend, Sir Martin Conway, the explorer, was with him on this jaunt.)

I shall always remember a most graphic description of his journey to Folkestone. He was on board a destroyer which had run into such heavy weather that it was impossible to enter harbour for fear of running aground. A small steamer was sent out to take him to shore. (He was Prime Minister at the time, incidentally.) A rope ladder was slung down to the swaying deck of the smaller vessel, and amidst tempestuous seas which swung it frantically, he insisted on being the first of his party to make the violent crossing. He was singing just as heartily on that occasion when he made the slippery descent to the other boat, lurching and swinging with the drunken rolling of the warship. Any moment he could have slipped from his precarious grip of the sodden oily rope, either to be dashed against the side of the ship or precipitated on the deck of the steamer. For him it was a delightful and memorable experience. When his secretary followed him he shouted up to him not to forget to take his umbrella. Sylvester took him at his word and descended, clutching it firmly!

Threats of assassination seemed to amuse him. When the Wheeldons were convicted of attempting to murder him during the war, he spoke kindly of them as misguided zealots. When the I.R.A. secret tribunal announced that they had sentenced him to death with other selected members of the British Government, he was the only one of the 'condemned' men who greeted the sentence with a roar of laughter.

During a stormy election, a drunken idiot hurled a burning paraffin-soaked faggot into his cab. It fell in my mother's lap and set fire to her dress. My father beat the flames out with his hands—and after seeing that mother was cared for, continued his electioneering.

His fondness of physical excitement and daring was matched by a love of the elements, of foreign parts. He was a great traveller and something of a mountaineer. His enthusiasms were a little disconcerting to his friends. During a journey in Switzerland on one occasion, he went round knocking on their bedroom doors at about four o'clock in the morning, and when the weary-eyed travellers opened up and demanded to know if a fire had broken out, they saw L. G. in tweeds, climbing boots and a shepherd's crook under his arm (!). 'All out!' he thundered. 'All out! We're going up the mountain to see the sunrise.'

He was an occupational golfer. By 'occupational' I mean that he played golf as other people draw aimless doodles on their blotting paper during serious conferences. It took the debating club out into the green fields, which was what the former country boy was really after. (Winston plays with bricks for the same reason, I've no doubt: mental relaxation.) L. G. was the only practitioner of the sport, however, who innocently caused the collapse of a government as a result of introducing the game to a fellow statesman, but this story I shall tell later. He was not at all bad at the game, but hardly as good as he supposed. It was rather like his fishing—he had a natural swing and could throw a line over the horizon, but he was a poor finisher.

His love of music was a serious thing. He disliked jazz, but his enthusiasm for classical music, particularly choral and church music, was absolutely genuine, and he was a connoisseur of the finest operatic works. It was heavenly to have some of the wonderful exponents—Melba, Patti and so on—for an evening with us; and I think they enjoyed them, too.

He was fond of pets. There was an Airedale, a fine brute, but something of a terror to comparative strangers to the home. There was Juan, the black cat, and Blanco, the white one. And Doodie, a tame white pigeon, presented to him on his American trip, who would caress his eyebrows after carefully removing his pince-nez (never attempting to peck his eyes), and then march down his shirt-front with an engaging comicality, crooning with satisfaction in the knowledge that he was the centre of attention. Doodie was let out of his cage every evening, but never tried to fly away. He was given the freedom of the house, and it was a little strange at times to see him sail into the drawing-room from the library, help himself to a cherry from a bowl and wing away. A visitor—new to the home—once swore that he was suffering under some sort of optical illusion, induced by the Welsh Wizard, who was playing a practical joke on him.

Father was both querulous and boastful—about small things. He complained frequently about inefficiencies in the management of the estate and farm—he himself always boasted he could do things twice as well in a tenth of the time. And whilst he was invariably modest about his parliamentary work, he boasted largely about his prowess as a golfer, a fisherman, a farmer, in fact about everything of which he was an amateur.

'Efficiency!' he demanded. It was one of his favourite words.

Managers and consultants of the estate and farm came and went. No one seemed to satisfy—his family least of all, whom he characterised roundly and generally as boobies.

He personally was about as inefficient as could be imagined, and in practical things he was quite inept. His secretaries dared not entrust him with any State document, because he had a habit of stuffing it into a pocket or a drawer or inside a book and then accuse them of losing it. The Irish settlement treaty—and heaven knows how many months of negotiation that entailed, and what measure of tears and blood stained it—'disappeared' for twenty-five years, and turned up again purely by chance when his personal effects were being itemised.

Nearly always he had to have somebody to help him dress. Faithful old Sarah, the housekeeper, would grumblingly bend down and tie up his bootlaces because she feared he would tie his feet together or something equally daft. The simplest mechanical gadget baffled him. There was a certain rather awkward door-handle which everyone else in the home had got used to. Whenever we heard a loud shout we suspected it was father, demanding help to have the door opened.

Well—that is a profile, a line drawing of the man, the lively, engaging, admirable, maddening and amusing personality. But it is a surface impression only to fill in the background of the stage props, cloak, flowing locks and mangold-wurzels. For the deeper image—that is the theme of this book.

4

FATHER was Chancellor, and this was an 'at home', with many glamorous visitors, including a red-headed lady.

When I first saw the lady, I was filled with admiration—a copper-tinted crown of rosettes, curlicues and ringlets. Mad Irish or wanton Spanish. Sumptuous brows, eyelashes thick as black crayon: a twenty-inch waist.

I followed her in secret rapture with my gaze to every part of the drawing-room, too nervous to ask for an introduction, waiting for a mutual friend to lead me to her.

A little later, out of the corner of my eye, I saw her depart through the french windows to the garden. It would not be too difficult to effect an introduction away from the crowd of guests. I put down my glass and sauntered in the direction of the french windows, pausing for a moment here and there to greet somebody, but making progress towards the exit. In the quiet garden she and I would be alone for a few minutes, perhaps.

Where did she come from? Who was she? Was she from Society or from what was known as Bohemian Society? An actress? An operatic singer? At least she was a beauty, and an artist. I was filled with romantic fancies.

At last I saw an opening in the crowd of guests, and slipped out into the garden. But the lady obviously did not want to be disturbed. Someone was already waiting for her. I recognised a very familiar figure, half turned from me.

He did not notice me; neither did she. They were deep in conversation which seemed too intimate to suffer disturbance. Father knew her, then.

I hung about in the doorway near the loggia, waiting for a glance in my direction which might break up the *tête-à-tête*. For some inexplicable reason, I was determined to hold my ground, not to be diverted. She was My Girl. I had picked her out. Father wasn't going to monopolise her. He had no Right, anyway.

Suddenly, he spun round. No one had warned him of my presence. She had not noticed me—and would not have cared if she had, it seemed. But some instinct had warned father that I was standing there, almost malevolently, patiently, vigilantly—demanding that the intimacy between them must end.

'Dick——' he said, quietly, dangerously. 'Don't just stand there. If you wish to be introduced to this lady——'

'I wondered if she cared to have some champagne,' I said with a youthful stubbornness.

They were silent, regarding me calculatingly. No introduction was offered, no answer was made to my curt invitation—and I retired, disturbed, incalculably angry, hardly able myself to recognise the cause for my violent feelings.

Then, a few moments later, as I bumped into one of mother's friends, I became aware of the reason for my disturbed state. No, it was not simple pique or jealousy of my father.

A little while ago I had seen this friend introduce the lady to father—and they had pretended not to have met before. This was the cause of my irritation: suspicion, pain. ('Don't hurt mamie.') A dozen different times—on every possible sort of occasion—wherever I turned, this sort of thing seemed to be happening.

Father was conducting intrigue after intrigue. Mutual friends, deep in conversation, would suddenly become silent as they saw me approach. When I entered a room and found father sitting there alone, deep in thought, he would start to protest loudly that I shouldn't 'creep in like that', as though he were trying to camouflage by noise some guilty thought that I could somehow overhear.

Was it imagination? Were all these indications misunderstood on my part? Had I grown into a dangerous habit of misjudging him? Did I have to interpret all his actions in terms of guilt? And were all my mother's tears at this time the overflow of too much jealousy? All three of us—mother, Olwen and I—had begun to condemn generally, see guilt all the time—and I was desperately trying not to be unfair, not to misjudge him.

My feelings about father's affairs with women vacillated, of course. Childish moral fervour yielded later to youthful cynicism and sophistication. There were the odd times when I considered him rather colourful and amusing in his gallantries. This state of mind was dependent upon the circumstances at the time, the sort of women who were involved with him and whether the affair had hurt mother or not. I sedulously avoided taking issue with him on this matter. I was afraid, I suppose, of revealing priggishness or sentimentality over mother. Gwilym appeared to notice very little—he was much younger—but Olwen was very sharp and observant (father always shied from introducing Olwen into his circle of feminine acquaintances).

In those pre-First World War days, the sense of leisure and elegance seemed to form a perfect setting for amorous adventures. Amongst our family friends were the most prominent socialites and wealthiest business men and industrialists. Wealth, as is well known, often attracts beauty.

I remember Lady J., married to an Australian mine owner. She was dark, tall and very attractive. In those days women wore extravagantly feminine clothes, with big picture hats and floral embellishments. They decked themselves with velvet and ivory and jade, all the textures that set off the feminine skin. There were lavish social occasions with receptions at gracious homes, with splendid gardens and terraces.

Amongst other invitations to the family I was sometimes asked with father to big houses in the country or near the river. Lady J.'s husband was one of the wealthy and it was very pleasant to be a guest in their home near Henley.

I myself had formed an admiration for Lady J., but was completely inhibited from expressing it by the fact that I was a guest enjoying her husband's hospitality. I could see that father shared my admiration, and one morning after breakfast in their home, we went for a stroll by the river and had a father-to-son talk about life and marriage and sex and so on. I was now old enough—in my early twenties—to be treated as an equal in the worldly sense. The conversation began with a discussion about Lady J.; and— after a few tentative exchanges in which we recognised an accord —I asked him frankly his views on sex and personal morality.

Father picked up a dead stick and tossed it into the river. The current gathered it up and sent it swinging along until it was out of sight.

'You see that? You can either go that way with the current or you can try to fight it. But if you decide to fight it you must be satisfied that you have a good reason for doing so. Do you understand me?'

'Are you talking about—women?' I said, hesitatingly.

'I am talking about love,' he corrected me.

'And how would you describe love?'

'That surely must be different for different people. Some have a very strong capacity for it. With others it's shallow and tepid.'

I know that he was trying to explain himself, to justify himself, but in the circumstances it was difficult and the generalities he talked in were not satisfactory.

I could not help thinking that this was paganism; but as I had never convinced myself that paganism was necessarily wrong in itself, I could not criticise the view expressed.

'There are some things which are wrong and some things which are obscene,' father said. 'For instance, if a very bloated old man manages to acquire a beautiful young wife because of his money, whether the match is solemnised in church or not, it is still in my opinion entirely immoral.'

It was well said and with a fine air of conviction; but I could not help taking quickly the implication of the remark—that as marriage in itself was not necessarily moral, it must follow therefore, according to this theory, that extra-marital relationships need not be immoral. It was on the tip of my tongue to challenge him on this, but I could not overcome my inhibition in view of our relationship.

It was an odd feeling walking beside my father that morning, each of us I am sure on the verge of some sort of deep, revealing confidence and neither of us quite having the emotional courage to break the barrier down. He made one final effort and said something to the effect that when one is mature and experienced the comfortable codes that one accepts as standard universal fixtures for one's conduct no longer appear quite so rigid or infallible.

What it was that prompted this exchange I am not sure. I had a vague thought that perhaps his mood was somehow more profound. Was it possible that he was really in love with someone—Lady J. perhaps? When I spoke about women he had answered with a reference to love. I was not sure what he meant by that; or whether his understanding of love was the same as mine.

I had tried to trace some sort of pattern in his affairs, if such a thing were possible and his was not the inconsequential behaviour of a bee gathering sweetness wherever it was available.

His way of life seemed to suggest the latter theory. I could certainly not recognise any pattern in his choice of partners, whose only common denominator seemed to be their human frailty.

At last I had the courage to pose a question to him, although in a humorous, indirect way. 'Do you believe that man is the pursuer or does he chase after the girl until she catches him?'

He smiled, and his magnificent bushy moustache bristled (it seemed to have an independent life of its own when he was pleased).

This indirect enquiry as to his views on Don Juanism seemed to appeal to him, and I could see him trying to make up his mind to give me an enthusiastically expressed view on this delectable topic, which he had obviously long studied.

'Nature,' he propounded, 'has selected the male as the active agent in the game of life, and I shall prove it to you, Dick. Let us imagine, for instance, fifty people marooned on a desert island. If the colony consists of one man and forty-nine women, there is no doubt that within a few generations there will be a thriving community of several hundred inhabitants. If, on the other hand, there were originally forty-nine men and only one woman, in six or seven generations there would only be a handful of cretinous or physically degenerate blood relatives.'

I worked it out and agreed that he was probably correct in his biological summary.

I told him that I had little doubt that he was right. 'But,' I said, 'as we are not on a desert island consisting of forty-nine women and one man or forty-nine men and one woman, I cannot see the value of this. On the contrary, for some peculiar reason known only to nature, every community seems to produce an equal number of males and females.'

Father offered no satisfactory reply to this and I did not note it in my jottings after our walk, but I have sometimes wondered since this memorable conversation whether he really and sincerely believed in this 'active agent' theory of his.

Later in the day I was strolling in the large grounds and I saw Lady J. sitting in a swing, flirtatiously poking father with her pointed shoe.

These were days of long skirts and it was rather daring for a lady to be seen in a swing at all; and when sitting in it it was proper to remain comparatively at rest. I saw father catch the heel, draw the lady back, then give a very hefty thrust. She shot away with a shriek and came sailing back over his head with a flurry of petticoats that would have done credit to a can-can expert. Her clear laughter rang out; there was not the slightest suspicion of rebuke in her voice.

The old boy looked round quickly, his moustache on end with vitality, and then turned to give the flying form another mighty push.

In the *Bystander* of July 29th, 1908, this paragraph appeared:

Mr Chancellor's Troubles

All is not going well with Mr Lloyd George in his new and exalted sphere. Not only is he having a most uncomfortable time of it politically, as a result of certain queer intrigues conducted by him and a certain colleague in connection with a proposed reduction of Army and Navy expenditure, but rumour is now busy as to the existence of embarrassment of another kind, which is even less likely to prove of assistance to his career. Mr George has, of course, been overloaded with flattery of late, especially from the fair sex, which is always difficult for a man of 'Temperament' to resist. The matter may, of course, be kept quiet. Also, it may not. *Nous verrons.*

The main heading of the article was worded significantly, *Indiscretions—Irish and Otherwise.*

Father brought a libel action, as he was bound to do, and the editorial board promptly got cold feet. An apology was printed on the 16th September, and a donation was sent to Caernarvon

Cottage Hospital of three hundred guineas at father's request. But this was by no means the end of the story. There was a spate of gossip in the clubs and drawing-rooms, and the *People* newspaper published a series of articles quite boldly giving details about an *affaire* involving Lloyd George and a jealous husband who was about to name him as co-respondent in a divorce suit, stating that desperate efforts were being made by Mr Lloyd George and his friends to buy out the would-be petitioner. In a final instalment, it was said that the 'price of peace' was determined in the sum of no less than twenty thousand pounds! The threatened petition was stayed.

Father took action again, briefing Rufus Isaacs, F. E. Smith and Raymond Asquith, suing the *People* for libel.

If the story were true, they still had no technical defence on their own account. If the outraged husband had been silenced with regard to his petition, then this silence would extend to any evidence he might be called to make for the *People* in support of the main contention of their story.

The defence would then be forced to plead cynically that they were unable to prove their story, but that they had acted in good faith, in the public interest, without malice and in the belief that they had presented the facts to their readers. The victory could only then be a technical one. Why should a large and disinterested newspaper like the *People* fabricate an attack on the reputation of the Chancellor of the Exchequer? The *People* editorial board had no personal enmity for the Chancellor. The issue would be unresolved even after the legal victory. The doubt would remain in the public mind. Had the story been true, then? And had the *People* been unable to prove its case because their witness had been bought off in the sum of twenty thousand pounds?

Father knew that win or lose, his career was greatly endangered. He had an unerring instinct about the public temper.

'You must stand by me, Maggie. Otherwise, it's all over with me.'

My father was forty-six, holding a post second in importance only to that of the Prime Minister. He knew that he would be attacked mercilessly if my mother expressed open doubt as to his innocence, if it were shown that she did not support him in his rejection of the accusation. There was great danger even if she remained uncommitted to his cause.

I know that my mother, a deeply religious woman, was in torment in giving support to the lie to be sworn on oath. As a woman, she had been mortally hurt by his infidelities. As a wife, she had been gravely wronged. I know exactly the extent of her conflict.

'You must help me, Maggie. If I get over this, I give my oath you shall never have to suffer this ordeal again.'

'You will go into the witness-box?'

'Yes.'

'And you will give your oath that this story is untrue?'

'I have to.'

'And you give *me* your oath that I shall not have to suffer this sort of thing again. How can I rely on your "oath"?'

'I can make it true. Maggie, I put my life in jeopardy for my beliefs. One day I shall be Prime Minister. I shall be a force for the public good. If you help me, you shall never regret your decision.'

My mother told me much about the conversations she had with father at this time. (She was never to forget them.) She did not want him to plead with her to save his career 'for the public good'. She did not care about that; she wanted simply to help him because he was hurt and frightened and in grave trouble. She could not deny him help then.

On the 12th March, 1909, the Chancellor of the Exchequer drove to the Law Courts in the Strand. As can be imagined, this was a gala day for every newspaper reporter, socialite and politician. My father's enemies had turned out in force. There were rumours that Mrs Lloyd George was leaving her husband, that papers had been submitted to solicitors. Her carriage, packed with trunks, had been seen bound for the station where she was to take the train to Criccieth. Others believed that she was at home, but estranged from her husband and waiting the outcome of the case before filing a suit against him.

Mr Lloyd George alighted from his car, and it was then seen that his wife had accompanied him. Together they entered the courtroom. Throughout the hearing she sat at his side.

Off duty: a game of golf with Megan on his 75th birthday (*above*). During the game
he remarked, 'Golf is good training for politicians—because it is full of bunkers.'
(*Below*) At home with Olwen and Megan.

The author.

He was called into the witness-box.

'Have you read the allegations made in the *People*?' his counsel asked him.

'Yes.'

'Are they true in substance or in fact?'

'The paragraphs are an absolute invention,' he said firmly, 'every line of them.'

Cross-examination?

None.

Carson, for the defence, offered a 'sincere and frank apology' for the allegations, saying that they were without foundation or justification.

The case was over, and damages to the plaintiff were put at a thousand pounds, a modest sum, indeed, for an 'unfounded and unjustified' attack on the reputation of the Chancellor of the Exchequer. But father was glad to settle the matter without further parley. This money, too, went to a local Welsh cause.

Even my father's worst enemies were silenced by mother's presence at his side during the hearing, and the anticipated aftermath of privileged sniping in the Commons did not take place; nor did anyone refer to the meagre estimate of damages awarded the Chancellor. The general feeling was that, innocent or not, if Maggie stood by him, that was good enough. The chapter was closed.

This is an appropriate point at which to say a few words about mother, the real heroine of this book.

One often assumes that in the life of a great man, the woman he married in his early days is necessarily a cipher, an insignificant creature, who fails to keep up with him in the stirring days of his great achievements. I think that the opposite is true in mother's case. Father had the brilliance and the energy for greatness, but not the sense of responsibility necessary to it. He was wayward, self-indulgent, spoiled and thoroughly reckless. In a dozen different ways, on innumerable occasions, mother's influence and support, her shrewdness and restraint, guided him through dangerous reefs of which the one I have described is merely the most theatrical. The hidden sources of his strength he drew from her. In his most dangerous days, during the anti-war campaign of the

Boer period, he could not possibly have continued his dedicated work without the support of her remarkable moral courage; and it was this period of his political life that was the most telling in establishing him as a dynamic force, a great personality and a born leader and crusader. It put him on the path to supreme leadership. In the dark days of the First World War, in the doldrum days, the days of deadlock, when the cry arose for a fighting man to rough-hew the national destiny, the leaders of all the parties deferred to Lloyd George because he had proved to them that he was capable of front-line courage as well as organisational genius.

This and much more he owed to her support; and it becomes all the more difficult to understand him so recklessly putting their marriage in hazard with these empty adventures. Not one of them could be dignified by the status of a grand *amour*. They were venal, all of them; they turned his head, sapped his will. And what happened when, driven finally beyond endurance, his wife left him?

5

'HAVE you ever thought how it felt to play God?' father said to me one day. 'The closest to this experience is being Chancellor of the Exchequer to the richest country on earth. Here you have all the wealth of mankind to draw on. You dispose of this or that—so much for necessities, so much for the needy, the sick and ailing. And an iron hand to master the strong, the selfish. But, *diuw*—that Budget speech! It nearly killed me. No one has ever invented a method to make figures sound dramatic. Tuppence on income tax—that's a battle cry that would have defeated Demosthenes!'

Lloyd George's Budget speech, which took some four hours, was a faltering, bumbling affair, in parts almost unintelligible and in others semi-coherent; but when he completed it the House knew that it was the most important ever delivered in the Commons. There were a large number of challenging issues, although these were acceptable, even the introduction of super-tax; but what astounded and terrified the powerful and privileged was an attack on the holiest bastion of property, a tax on land.

The ducal landlords in London, permanently entrenched members of a privileged society, regarded this tax as an encroachment on their most jealously guarded and most lucrative source of income. Lloyd George's arguments had the most powerful impact on the country as a whole. Land originally granted to families at three or four pounds an acre in time became worth five, six, seven *thousand* pounds an acre, and still remorselessly growing as the industrial might of London increased the value of the property. And the dukes were the only members of the community who had contributed nothing to this increase in value. Small wonder that there was such agitation and heart-burning anguish over such a tax. Lloyd George had touched on a very sensitive part of the ducal conscience.

The outcry in high places was tumultuous. This upstart, this nobody from the backwoods, this Welsh foster-son of a shoemaker had the temerity to tamper with the inherent, sacrosanct interests of his betters. But they would teach him. Even if the Conservatives were out of office, they still ruled, was the grim reminder. The House of Lords would not pass such an Act. Neither did they. After scores of stormy debates in the Commons, it was pushed through to the Lords, where it was rejected.

Lloyd George watched this lordly manœuvre with malevolent relish. The gauntlet was down. He would show his peers a bit of rural in-fighting which the Marquess of Queensberry had not dreamed of in framing his sporting code.

A sinister rumour began to sound in the lobbies that the Chancellor had proposed a remarkable policy for the Lords. No, he was not going to try to abolish them. That would have taken a generation. He had an odder, more astonishing and very humiliating project in mind. The government of course had, in practice, the power to create new peers. What Mr Lloyd George now proposed to the Cabinet was that three *hundred* new peers be created, sympathetic to the Liberal Party, to swamp the Conservative opposition in the Lords. This early bit of political ju-jitsu was typical of my father's mental processes in politics as well as other matters. Here was this crusader against the Lords blandly proposing to swell their ranks so that their own strength could be turned against them. He had this ability to think at a tangent to the normal line, and very rewarding it would be at times.

The psychological effect of such rumours—and he did in fact propose this scheme to the Cabinet—had exactly the sort of profoundly disturbing result he had hoped for. It completely demoralised the run-of-the-mill Conservative peer, who imagined his future colleagues would be recruited from dockers, miners, anarchists, ex-Boer Commandos, Irish terrorists and revolutionary-syndicalists. And with my father's truculent sense of humour, I am not altogether sure they were wrong. He told me later that there was never much serious intent in his proposal. He wanted the rumour to get about, though, that the Cabinet would start taking steps to frame such a policy. It would be enough to 'put a scare' into the Lords and weaken them for the second assault on their veto.

My father thoroughly enjoyed these running feuds with the Lords. He had always to have some sort of opposition to whet his steel on—whether it was the Bishop of St Asaph, 'Brummagem' Joe Chamberlain or the Lords—the bigger they are, the harder they fall, as has been observed.

In any case, the Lords were battleship-sized targets without the gunnery equipment of such giants. What superb ammunition Lord Rosebery's remark provided for him! That worthy had aired his views about L. G.'s proposed old age pensions for people over 69 (five shillings a week *maximum*, going down to one shilling a week according to other means, was the proposal—and it was pointed out that as things stood at the time hardly anyone would ever grow old enough to enjoy these benefits in the prevailing conditions of malnutrition amongst the working classes). 'Such prodigality,' solemnly propounded his lordship, referring to this pension scheme, 'might well deal a blow to the Empire from which it might not recover.' L. G. gave his listeners a few facts and figures—three ducal landlords between them drawing rents totalling £354,000 per annum was one example.

He kept up a running barrage of threats, jeers, denunciations inside the House and on public platforms from Limehouse to Llanystumdwy which never gave the noble members an undisturbed night's rest for months.

The Tory Press had screamed as loudly as the Lords—they were all hurt in the place it hurts them most, their pockets—and had described him as a highwayman, a robber, a pirate and every other sort of brigand; and he revelled in his rôle. 'I would dearly like to rest,' he said, at the height of the gruelling campaign, 'but I prefer to fight.'

He tore into his foes: 'A bull in a china shop is much better as beef,' he said with sinister joviality. 'We have heard a great deal about self-government for Ireland. For Wales. Even for Scotland. But what about self-government for England? We are not allowed it. There are five or six hundred gentlemen—I beg your pardon, *Noble*men who wish to govern. What, if not whom, do they represent? They do not even represent Wealth as a whole.'

To the claim that the House of Lords was the 'watchdog of the constitution', he riposted with savage humour: 'You mean a poodle. It fetches and carries for Mr Balfour.'

And: 'It is easier for a rich man to enter the House of Commons than the Kingdom of Heaven. But easier still to enter the House of Lords. You have only to arrange to be born.'

The Duke of Beaufort declared that he would like to see Mr Lloyd George and his friend, Mr Winston Churchill, 'in the middle of twenty couples of dog hounds'.

King Edward also was upset. He had demurred and objected to the firebrand Liberal's appointment as Chancellor of the Exchequer, and his early fears were continually reinforced. He repeatedly expressed his displeasure that his influential minister—in such a position of responsibility—should so ally himself with subversiveness of established institutions.

Lloyd George wrote to the King at length, explaining that he had merely been defending himself against the severest form of attack on his considered policy. For himself, he was only concerned with effecting a harmonious and pacific solution to the controversy. All Mr Lloyd George wanted really was for everyone to be quiet and content.

And then he returned to the dukes. 'It costs twice as much to maintain a duke as a fully equipped battleship,' he explained to his listeners. 'Well, perhaps that is just. They are twice as terrible and last rather longer.'

In the midst of all this, there were the Suffragettes, that band of hysterical, neurotic or near-neurotic martyrs or would-be martyrs who heckled, smashed windows, undermined platforms, chained themselves to railings, attacked ministers on the golf course, set fire to the contents of pillar boxes, went to prison, suffered hunger strikes and marched, marched, marched against Authority. All the members of the government were their targets, including Mr Lloyd George, who was nursing a cherished policy to give them peacefully and without the least struggle what they were determined to fight and die for.

The tragedy about the Suffragettes was just that: their struggle probably delayed women's franchise by six or seven years, and when they finally got the vote they used it, in their feminine way, to help remove from office the government which agreed to give it to them and brought in the government which had opposed giving it to them. Yet the Suffragettes did not much disturb the hero of the Lloyd George Nights who had safely survived the Battle of Birmingham Town Hall.

In February 1910 Lloyd George and his colleagues were ready to make their second assault on the Lords' veto. The House approved resolutions to exclude the Lords from interfering with a Money Bill of any description and preventing them from vetoing any Bill whatever more than twice. The Prime Minister warned the Lords that if they refused to pass the Bill, there would be Consequences.

The memory of the previous threats made tangible past fears. Lloyd George's 'People's Budget', with its family tax allowances and super-tax and land tax, was passed through both Houses without further difficulty.

Looking back historically, it is ironic to note that the really significant items, such as super-tax, had not met with any special opposition; and these were the important social policies—the first break through on the Welfare Front, first minor adjustments of economic injustice which were to establish a precedent for future legislation on a formidable scale—sixpence in the pound after £5,000 a year for super-tax. Today it starts at a far lower figure and goes up to eighteen shillings in the pound. On the other hand, the burning issue of the land tax, which struck terror into the mighty and privileged, turned out to be a very minor measure in practice, drawing very little revenue for the Exchequer. But though the Lords' and Dukes' fire was misdirected, their fears were justified.

Workmen's compensation, old age pensions, widows' pensions, the Seamen's Charter, unemployment insurance—these were policies Lloyd George had either successfully fought or was fighting for; and whilst he gave with one hand he took with the other. Soak the Rich! A 'Robbers' Budget', shrieked the Dukes. 'Thou Shalt Not Steal', screamed the posters on the brewers' vans. The City was in uproar.

Thus dawned the century of the common man, and Lloyd George was its first active sponsor.

In his struggles, L. G. had staunch support from the Prime Minister. He told me what a ferocious contest each Budget measure invoked in the Cabinet. Asquith leaned back comfortably in the Chair and when the contestants turned in desperation to him for a ruling, he would say, 'Well, there seems to be substantial agreement with Mr Chancellor's proposal. Next item . . .?' The least effective support came from John Burns, that fogged and bewildered former Labour agitator. 'I hope,' father said to me one day, 'I don't get paralysis of the pistol after a few years of "success". Poor old John Burns lost his ammunition the first time a duke invited him to tea. I relied on him, but there was nothing there. What happens to human beings? To me, he had once been a hero.'

'Four spectres haunt the poor,' Lloyd George thundered. 'Old age, Accident, Sickness and Unemployment. We are going to exorcise them. We are going to drive hunger from the hearth. We mean to banish the workhouse from the horizon of every workman in the land.'

He was not the only one who raised his voice against the appalling conditions which so arbitrarily divided society in those days. Ben Tillet, who helped to win the Docker's Tanner and whose mighty orations on Tower Hill were preceded by this fervent prayer, 'Dear God, strike Lord Devonport dead!' wanted a genuine Soviet; Tom Mann, who went to prison for his historic pamphlet, 'Don't Shoot!' addressed to the soldiers called out to face the industrial rioters; Jim Larkin, who said that he was dedicated to the divine proposition of stirring up discontent. These were some of the more tumultuous voices raised in protest; but all of them today are remembered only by the dreamers of revolutionary change. The aged and the widows who draw their pensions from the post office, the injured working-men, the sick— all these who obtain practical help for their sustenance and succour, in their millions, are the legatees of Lloyd George's working policies, remorseless scheming and campaigning against Authority in its every form.

There was the Insurance Act of 1911, passed in the face of opposition from almost everyone concerned in it—the doctors, the employers, the apathetic multitudes for whose benefit it was hammered into shape—the rock of opposition its anvil.

A cartoon showed a furious duchess protesting, 'What! Me lick stamps?' The *Daily Mail* inflamed the tempers of its readers with warnings that their homes would be invaded by Mr Lloyd George's inspectors demanding to see that the cards were in order; and the servant girls were warned that their mistresses would sack them the moment they became eligible for sickness pay.

In this spirit of outraged privilege, the Conservative Ladies hired the Albert Hall for a mass demonstration. Some ten thousand of them packed the building, singing 'Taffy was a Welshman, Taffy was a Thief'. 'Guillotiner', 'Tyrant', 'Gagger', they chanted; and then, happily relieved by this mass catharsis of the appalling imposition of having to pay threepence a week to insure their wretchedly underpaid drudges for medical help, they returned to their limousines and drove home.

One of the very nastiest manifestations of reaction in its extremist form is demonstrated by these Ladies in full battle cry. Anyone who has seen them protesting in mass meetings against the abolition of capital punishment or the Cat, screaming for the Birch, in paroxysms of terror that this implement will be done away with, can testify to the horrific spectacle of frustrated sexuality in its direst form.

Lloyd George used to make jokes about the Ladies, but one way or another, they, too, almost cost him his life. The less misguided members of the sex were not the least dangerous. The 'Servants Tax Resisters Defence League' worked off steam at the Albert Hall, but the militant Suffragettes expressed their hysteria by planting a bomb in our home, which wrecked four rooms. Fortunately, no one was in at the time, and maybe the women who planted it had planned it that way, blowing up almost half the furniture merely as a warning. Mrs Pankhurst took responsibility for this crass piece of criminality. She was tried at the Old Bailey, convicted and sentenced to three years' penal servitude. She immediately went on hunger strike. 'What an extraordinary mixture of idealism and lunacy!' father said, when he heard of the sentence. 'Hasn't she the sense to see that the very worst way of campaigning for the franchise is to try to intimidate or blackmail a man into giving her what he would gladly give her otherwise?' He felt very sorry for her.

One of the women threw a steel spike through the window of father's cab. It missed his eye by a fraction and pierced his cheek. 'Now, I simply *can't* do anything for them at the present,' he fumed in exasperation. 'Why on earth don't they try a normal piece of feminine blandishment!' He grinned through his wounded face, and I'm sure he was picturing a recruitment of accomplished siren-toned Mata Haris to undermine his resistance. I could have told them that this would have been a far more potent technique of campaigning.

I remember going up to my room one evening at No. 11 and finding that the light bulb had 'gone'. In a fit of exasperation and youthful thoughtlessness I tossed it out of the window into the street. The subsequent explosion on our front doorstep brought the police in squads to our defence, causing terror amongst certain innocent female passers-by. I hurried to procure their release! I blush at the memory.

Lloyd George's successes in his programme of social reform excited him into the formulation of yet more ambitious projects; schemes for land reform, even rationalisation of industry. First of all, he studied every practical aspect of these problems. He was a great Eclectic. He was quite willing to borrow from the Labour reformers, the Webbs, the Fabians. Even on his travels abroad when he was officially on holiday he would make time to study social conditions and legislation. Thus, in Canada he found educational systems of a progressive nature which excited his admiration. In Germany, in Switzerland, there were advanced techniques of social service. He was as indefatigable as a squirrel planning for the winter, tapping each nut to test the soundness of its kernel before adding it to the store.

What further practical measures might he have introduced had it not been for the war!

*　　*　　*　　*

The relationship between Lloyd George and the King has caused a great deal of perplexity over the years.

In a speech at Oxford Lloyd George delivered one of his most forceful attacks on the House of Lords and, it seemed through some oratorical compulsion, he linked the King's name with that of the institution under assault.

King Edward was concerned and angry and the Prime Minister received a letter from Lord Knollys (December 3rd, 1906) which read as follows:

Dear Sir Henry,

The King desires me to point out to you that Mr Lloyd George brought in His Majesty's name in the speech which he made against the House of Lords at Oxford on Saturday.

The King sees it is useless to attempt to prevent Mr Lloyd George from committing breaches of good taste and propriety by abstaining from attacking, as a Cabinet Minister, that branch of the legislature, though His Majesty has more than once protested to you against them. . . .

But His Majesty feels that he has a right, and it is one on which he intends to insist, that Mr Lloyd George shall not introduce the Sovereign's name into these violent tirades of his, and he asks you as Prime Minister to be so good as to take the necessary steps to prevent a repetition of this violation of constitutional practice, and of good taste.

The King says he has no doubt he shall be told that it was only a 'phrase' but he must really make a point of his name being omitted, even from a 'phrase' in Mr Lloyd George's invective against the House of Lords.

Believe me, yours very truly,

Knollys.

The passage complained of seems at first reading to be a rather harmless one. Lloyd George had said in his speech:

'I think that the time has come, if the House of Lords insists on maintaining a claim to reject legislation that comes from the representatives of the people, to consider another great question. If a dissolution comes sooner or later, it will be, in my judgment, a much larger measure than the Education Bill that will come up for consideration, if the House of Lords persists in its present policy. It will come on an issue of whether this country is to be governed by King and Peers or by the King and his People.'

The average reader might find it puzzling that the King should have reacted so strongly against this relatively innocuous reference to his name. It was clear from the speech that the Monarchy was not being attacked, nor the institution of Monarchy; and I later discussed this matter with father to try to understand the underlying cause, if any, for this strong royal rebuke.

His explanation to me was a revelation of the subtlety and technique of propaganda.

'King Edward believed that the average person hearing or reading my speech would, as likely as not, confuse the words or transpose them slightly and believe that the Monarchy was being attacked as well as the institution of the Peers. What I said, of course, was, "It will come on an issue of whether this country is to be governed by King and Peers or by the King and his People". If someone mishears the words or fails to hear the end of the sentence; or if a reporter slightly misquotes the words, then there appears to be a direct attack on the Monarchy. I am afraid that King Edward thought I might have done this deliberately for some subversive reason.

'In fact, I was trying to do the opposite. This particular statement brought in the King's name in order to make it plain that I was making a distinction between the institution of Monarchy and the Lords. Had I simply launched an attack on the Lords it might have been understood by my listeners to mean that I was attacking the whole aristocratic hierarchy, including the royal family. That of course was not my intention.'

The Prime Minister, Sir Henry Campbell-Bannerman, tried to clear up the misunderstanding in his letter to the King's secretary:

4th December, 1906

Dear Lord Knollys,

I deeply regret to learn that the words of one of the King's Ministers have been such as to give offence to His Majesty, and on receipt of your letter I took the earliest occasion to see Mr Lloyd George.

As you are aware I had previously remonstrated with him as to his previous utterances in which he seemed to exceed his usual traits in condemning the actions of the House of Lords and in assailing the constitutional position of that House. . . .

Mr Lloyd George assures me that, bearing in mind the warning and rebuke of the former occasion, he endeavoured to be moderate on Saturday and I think he did not at least greatly err. . . .

I pointed out to him that His Majesty was chiefly annoyed by his introduction of the King's name which it was of course entirely improper to bring in, as making His Majesty in some sense a participator in a political controversy.

I presume that the passage referred to was that in which he said that it was not right to be governed by 'the King and the Peers'; he would bow to 'The King and the People.' He explained to me that he would have considered it would be disrespectful to speak of 'The Peers' alone and 'The People' alone, omitting a reference to the Supreme Head of the State; and he therefore used the phrase reported out of respect without the slightest idea of implying any connivance or co-operation; and that it was so understood.

Mr Lloyd George begged me to lay before the King the expression of his profound regret if he had inadvertently offended, and I would simply express the hope that His Majesty will, in view of the great tension of opinion and following which this keen controversy has evoked, look with indulgence on any indiscretion which might have been committed. . . .

Believe me, yours very truly,
H. Campbell-Bannerman.

My father's 'firebrand' activities, with his Insurance Bill and other measures of social reform, had made him extremely unpopular with established society and this, too, caused certain tensions in his relationship with the King. (It was even said later by some of the Tories that Lloyd George had caused the King's early death through worry, but this was absolute nonsense, because King Edward, who had undergone a dangerous operation for appendicitis before his Coronation, had since that time never been a well man.)

I remember once asking father, with the somewhat disconcerting logic that seems to be characteristic of the young, whether he really believed in the monarchy as an institution in view of his scathing comment about the Lords that all they required, in the way of qualification for their high status, was to be born. 'Wouldn't that apply equally to the King?' I demanded.

Father treated the question quite seriously and explained it to me satisfactorily. 'My quarrel with the Lords is that they are an adjunct of the Conservative Party. The monarchy is an independent institution and the King undoubtedly has a useful purpose as a sort of paterfamilias for all the children of the Empire. Even grown-ups are really children, Dick, and I think that republicans, too, have to glorify the personality of their president or political leader.'

He was thinking of Americans and of the fantastic and exaggerated regard they have for aristocratic titles; but years later I recalled his argument when I learned that the film of the Coronation of Queen Elizabeth was the most popular cinematic offering shown in Soviet Russia.

In spite of the tensions between King Edward and Lloyd George —the King wrote frequently to the Prime Minister about the dangers of Mr Chancellor's pronouncements—they became quite good friends in a way. Edward had a sense of humour and personally they rather liked each other.

During his chancellorship father was asked to visit the King at Balmoral. It was at the very height of his social and political unpopularity but King Edward behaved in a hospitable and cordial way; and a dinner party father attended there proved to be a very pleasant affair, including the royal family, with Queen Alexandra, the Prince of Wales (who later of course became George V) and the Princess.

Later in the evening, when the port was circulating and everyone was in a mellow mood, King Edward said to the Prince, 'George, you must tell the story about the gold medal winner that you told the other day—you know, the fellow who saved somebody from drowning in the canal.'

'No, no, I can't do that,' the Prince protested.

'You must,' the King insisted humorously. 'You may regard it virtually as a command!'

'Oh, very well then,' the Prince said in mock resignation. 'It appears that a man was recently awarded a gold medal for life-saving. He was walking along beside a canal when he saw a drowning man thrashing about in the water. He jumped in and after a great struggle brought him to safety. The hero was later identified and a medal was presented to him by the Lord Mayor. After the presentation the Lord Mayor said: "That was a very gallant deed, you must tell us how it happened." "Well, ladies and gentlemen," said the hero, "I saw this man struggling in the water, face downwards and obviously in difficulties. I jumped in, turned him over and—when I saw that it wasn't Mr Lloyd George—I brought him to shore." '

Some of my earliest interesting memories at home in Downing Street were Prince Edward's occasional visits. He was about fifteen years of age and taking lessons in the Welsh language from father before his investiture at Caernarvon as Prince of Wales.

He was a shy, quiet boy—I remember his strict upbringing by a father who believed in naval discipline—and I think that he was pleasantly surprised at the relaxed family atmosphere, the easy relationship between children and parents, in the Lloyd George household. He was the same age as Gwilym, and I remember thinking what a contrast this quiet boy appeared to be to my brother, who combined the normal boisterousness with lack of inhibition. We all became good friends and father developed a warm regard for him which endured throughout the years.

In the long dining-room at No. 11, father would ask him to stand at one end, throw out his chest and repeat the sonorous Welsh phrases so that they could be clearly heard at the other.

Occasionally he would call one of us in to stand beside Prince Edward and join him in a chorus.

What a Welsh teacher Prince Edward had in Lloyd George!

'Yes, there's a lilt in the pronunciation but you must remember that Welsh is the language of bards and warriors. You need not be surprised that the words are sung.'

Whether or not Prince Edward proved to be an apt pupil I cannot now recall, but I remember him as a bright youngster with a lively and curious mind. Coming up the main staircase to father's room he once paused before the gallery of portraits of famous prime ministers. 'Who are these chaps?' he asked me (or words to that effect).

'They're the great prime ministers of England, Pitt, Walpole, Disraeli, and so on.'

'Yes, but what did they do? What were they famous for?' he insisted.

So before his next visit I hastily made reference and refreshed my memory, and gave him some rapid, potted biographies, to which he listened with quite eager interest. Then he said calmly, 'You've covered most of it, but there're a few other things which you've overlooked. I read about them all when I got home.'

His visits established warm and memorable personal links with our family and many years later, during the constitutional crisis over Mrs Simpson, father was gravely upset at his treatment by Baldwin and the others who compelled his abdication.

'It is true that the country is entitled to choose its monarch,' Lloyd George said, 'but the King is entitled to choose his own queen.'

I am sure that had father been prime minister at the time some other solution to the problem would have been found to spare his old friend and former pupil the unhappiness and humiliation which he suffered in those days.

On the Christmas Eve after the Abdication he sent the ex-King a telegram:

> Best Christmas greetings from an old minister of the Crown, who holds you in as high esteem as ever and regards you with deep and loyal affection, deplores the mean and unchivalrous attacks upon you and regrets the loss sustained by the British Empire of a monarch who sympathised with the lowliest of his subjects.

On Christmas Day he received this reply:

> Very touched by your kind telegram and good wishes which I heartily reciprocate. Edward. Cymru am byth! (Wales for ever!)

6

OUR home was the meeting ground of the high and the
mighty. When I think of this, I remember first of all the
Breakfasts. The Breakfasts were as famous as any royal
levée. They started off rather as a joke because father, who always
woke very early—about six o'clock—was fully alert and lively
by nine. (He had already done a couple of hours' work in bed
before going down to have his first meal of the day.) This
naturally gave him a singular advantage first thing in the morning, in any discussion or battle of wits. And politically he never
failed to use an advantage. So he invited Them to Breakfast.

They were the political bigwigs, the famous lawyers, business
men and newspapermen of his day. And there they were, at home
with the family, clinking tea-cups on saucers and fastidiously
nibbling toast with us, often very depressed by the dynamic
presence of their host. Not always, of course. Some of them were
tigers, too.

As a youngster I privately classified them into two categories:
the Dukes and the Marmadukes. This was my personal image, of
course, and I kept it strictly to myself. The 'Dukes' were the
genuine Greats—polished, urbane, immensely authoritative and
resourceful and always great personalities. The 'Marmadukes',
however, were the strutters and preeners, the spurious Dukes; in
fact, they were non-Dukes. I think I became quite adept at sizing
them up over the years; and checking later with father, I flatter
myself that many original impressions were justified. Needless to
say, the Dukes were not real dukes, although many real dukes
would be reckoned as nothing higher than a Marmaduke by my
appraisal.

There was a final, supreme category, the Archduke; but so few
of them attained this high eminence that several years would
elapse before I would mentally doff my hat in such company, and

for long periods I would forget this extra refinement of classification.

As I have little recollection of the Marmadukes now, and in any case as the reader would hardly find them either interesting or edifying, feelings can fortunately be spared in these random sketches which are confined only to Dukes and the occasional, rare Archduke—the reader will have to judge the form for himself.

F. E. Smith—later Lord Birkenhead. 'Galloper' Smith, he was called. And a very dashing personality; witty (to the point of folly), engaging and tremendously charming. I was a little shocked at an early meeting.

We were at breakfast at No. 11 when F. E. joined us. He was on his way to the Old Bailey to defend Ethel Le Neve, Crippen's girl friend and *femme fatale*, who was being tried as an accessory for the murder of his wife.

F. E. was in good humour and seemed to take his sombre task with a certain lightness which I found perturbing.

'May I borrow your Bible?' he asked me. 'I want to look up that bit about the woman taken in adultery.'

I told him that our family Bible would not be of much help to him, and he laughed and asked me if I would be good enough to borrow Mr Asquith's. I went along to the Prime Minister next door on my odd early morning errand.

'Is she guilty?' I asked F. E. with concern, handing him the Book.

'Not if I get her off,' he said amiably.

'I can't understand the man,' I told father, when he had gone. 'How can he joke about a thing like that? After all, she's on trial for her life.'

'If you can't learn to make jokes, you'll drown in the tears,' he said, with one of his remote smiles.

I never again questioned a criminal lawyer's sense of humour.

F. E. could never resist making a joke. One of them was said to have cost him an inheritance. He had been befriended by a right-wing Tory shipowner, a very wealthy man, who had mentioned him in his will. Rather vain, the old fellow was particularly proud of a beard which he kept well toned with artificial aid. At a dinner party, F. E. called him 'the original Dye-hard', a joke that went the rounds, and lost him a handsome sum of money.

He was one of the most brilliant men ever to grace the Bar and was probably the ablest impromptu speaker of his day. He obtained from father his most remarkable 'brief'. L. G. was at the Genoa Conference at the time and very hard-pressed with important meetings. Birkenhead walked into the hotel where the British delegates were staying. He was on holiday and wore a yachting cap and flannels.

'Just the man I want,' father said to him. 'I have twenty dozen meetings to fit in. Can you hold a Press conference on my behalf?'

'What's your case?'

Father told him. Birkenhead listened carelessly, without taking a single note. Then he sauntered off in his blazer and yachting cap to address a gathering of several hundred of the world's leading newspapermen. He gave what has been described as the most brilliant speech heard at the Conference, and then answered dozens of questions fired at him by these experts.

He was something of a practical joker, too. He invited a number of friends to dine with him on his yacht. Amongst these was Sir Philip Sassoon, who was such a poor sailor that he only agreed to come provided the boat stayed in harbour. The undertaking was given, but half-way through the meal, the sound of the engines started and the boat began to lurch. Sir Philip leaped to his feet, took a couple of chairs in his stride and vaulted over a table to reach the gangway—only to discover that the boat was still secured.

Sir Philip was never to survive his reputation as a hurdler.

A drink with father once cost F. E. a thousand pounds. He was present at the final meetings with the Irish leaders. Father had been exercising his guile, his hot and cold technique with the delegates that finally compelled them to come to terms. The experience was a most harrowing one, and when the agreement was at long last concluded, F. E. asked for a shot of whisky.

'Haven't you made a bet that you won't touch liquor for twelve months?' father reminded him.

'Yes. A thousand pounds. And I've only got a fortnight to go. Make it a double.'

That was F. E. Smith, Lord Birkenhead.

Sarah, our housekeeper, was answering the phone. 'Mr Lloyd George you want? Well, who wants him? Who? Northcliffe? Well, Mr Lloyd George is taking a nap. Can't you let the poor man have his rest?'

Northcliffe, 'King of Fleet Street'. A brooding, pugnacious character. Thoroughly hardbitten, arrogant, frequently at odds with father, who caustically described a conversation with him as 'like taking a walk with a grasshopper'. (Northcliffe never forgave him.)

He stalked in one day to father's offices. J. T. Davies, father's secretary, rose hastily to show him into father's room. 'No. I don't care whether I see him or not. A message will do. Tell him I hear that he's been trying to interfere with strategy. If he continues, I'll break him.' And he walked off.

Yes, let battle royal commence. L. G. cordially detested and greatly respected his adversary, who was 'the only man in England who tried to dictate policy to the British Prime Minister', he once told me.

On that occasion, he got a taste of his own arrogant thunder. L. G. sent him an open telegram, rejecting certain accusations about foreign policy, which ended with the words, 'Don't be always making mischief'. A bitter pill for the King of Fleet Street to swallow.

The only times I ever saw him I was too scared of him to exchange a word. His presence often seemed to brood in our home, and father had a special tone of voice in speaking of him.

Yet when father was in misery over the harassing Marconi affair, Northcliffe's Press almost alone in Fleet Street refrained from adding to the snarling tones of his accusers. For all his arrogance, Northcliffe was a man of considerable integrity. Father said to me in a tense moment of anxiety before the official enquiry, 'Your friends and your enemies. Judge them in the light and you will be deceived. You can only judge them in the hours of darkness.'

Northcliffe, a rare visitor, seemed to leave a ghost behind. What a contrast to the gaiety of F. E.!

Bonar Law. A mysterious, quiet, dry character. I could never tell what he was thinking. He would sit and listen to father by the hour, delicately non-committal and almost entirely monosyllabic. When he left, father would say, 'Brilliant chap. Most intelligent. After a discussion with him I always see things more clearly.'

(Harold Macmillan once said of Bonar Law that he 'acted on Lloyd George like water on brandy'. This is amusing, but it is not quite accurate. Bonar Law was more like the steering wheel to Lloyd George's hundred horse-power engine. A mildly raised eyebrow, a faintly sceptical intonation of voice, and the runaway fire-engine that was my father's political or strategic train of thought would be subtly deflected.)

'Bonar is wonderful'; 'Bonar is my best friend'; 'Thank God for Bonar'. These and similar fervent avowals of appreciation I often heard.

'You know, he's a curious and mysterious chap,' father chuckled, and told a story.

He was driving with Bonar and they were 'discussing' more general matters. That is, father was doing the 'discussing' and Bonar the listening. Father told him about a concert he had heard the previous evening and eloquently described the merits of the performances.

'I don't much care for music,' Bonar Law said.

A little later they passed some rather attractive scenery and over this, too, L. G. expressed himself with lyrical fervour.

'I don't greatly care for scenery,' Bonar murmured.

A little farther on they passed a group of women.

'Rather handsome, don't you think?' L. G. said.

'I'm not very interested in females,' said Bonar.

'Well, then—tell me, Bonar. Is there anything you *do* like?'

'Yes,' said Bonar. 'Bridge.'

A very mild and modest person, Bonar, with one special gift: the common touch. He had none of father's brilliance, but he did teach father a trick or two. In his speeches, when he wished to make some special point, he would pause, take out a notebook to which he would refer significantly and then slowly put it away, keeping his audience in deep suspense for the anticipated gem of argument. In fact, the notebook contained nothing.

A loyal friend and ally, 'meekly ambitious' but completely conscientious. When he was offered the premiership in the critical change-over during the war, he said, 'No. I promised it to Lloyd George. He's the man.'

Max Aitken, later Lord Beaverbrook.

He reminded me vaguely of a dynamic Chinese mandarin. He had a humorous, puck-like expression which belied the words he spoke, which were forceful, positive, even ruthless. A tireless, devoted, almost obsessive Imperialist, combining subtlety with strength of character. To befriend him would ensure championship in any crisis.

Father got his support in the tussle for the premiership during the war years, and spoke of him affectionately as the 'greatest direct-action specialist next to me'! Max's manoeuvrings certainly proved a boon to father.

He was a particular and warm friend of Bonar Law. Father told how Bonar had asked Aitken his opinion as to whether certain shares he had bought were likely to rise in value. 'They will,' said Aitken. They did. Aitken saw to it personally. He sent his brokers into the Stock Exchange arena and they bought such mighty blocks of the shares that the price shot up. His friend, who was seriously ill at the time, was thus ensured comfort and peace of mind.

Father made Beaverbrook Minister of Information in his government, and the irrepressible Max tried vainly to reconcile his political personality with his journalistic ego. Things began to hum when the *Daily Express*, owned by the Minister of Information, got a scoop which appeared to be due to Beaverbrook's inside knowledge. Later it turned out to be the independent work of one of his enterprising newspapermen. Beaverbrook loyally supported his staff-man, who was obviously entitled to publish a good newspaper story even if the owner of his paper was sitting, as it were, in the opposite camp.

Father was furious with Beaverbrook until I asked him what

he would have done in Beaverbrook's position. 'The same, of course!' he snorted. 'But if he were Premier he would be just as angry as I am. Don't try to mix me up, Dick!'

Later, things got much worse. Beaverbrook started to attack the government (which he still represented as a minister) in his own newspaper. The dual personality rôle was proving too much for him. Father's tantrums reduced me to helpless laughter, which added to his wrath until in the end he broke down and began to laugh too. His sense of high comedy was equal to any situation short of plain tragedy. In the years that followed I have always pictured Beaverbrook wielding a ministerial blue pencil in one hand and his crusader sword in the other. No doubt he sometimes used the one to sharpen the other.

And I never forgot father's description of him as a direct-action specialist. In the Second World War, as Minister for Aircraft Production, he was the most dynamic force in the government—next to Winston, this time.

Rufus Isaacs. A very dear friend. A warm and charming person, with a legal mind like a stiletto. As a boy of fifteen, he ran away to sea on a sailing-ship. One of his ports of call was Bombay. The next time he set foot in Bombay it was as Viceroy of India.

In a court of law, with such competition as Marshall Hall himself, he never failed to dominate; and his grasp of detail was so phenomenal that he could proceed effortlessly from courtroom to courtroom, dealing simultaneously with three or four involved commercial cases at once.

He was concerned in the wretched Marconi affair, and was himself subjected—the greatest cross-examiner of his day—to two whole days of cross-examination.

I asked him some time later about it. 'How did you feel?' I said with youthful impetuosity.

'Vastly interested. I wouldn't have missed the experience for worlds. I had often wondered what a witness feels at the receiving end. Now I know.'

'And what did you feel?'

'Guilty,' he said, grinning.

For all his precision-finished mental processes, Rufus Isaacs was a most romantic man temperamentally. He became very senti-mental when he received his appointment as Viceroy and pic-tured very lyrically a new mode of life. His fanciful description of it might have come straight out of Omar Khayyám. I would not attempt to reproduce it from memory!

What a contrast to Sir John Simon, another great lawyer, another mental calculating machine. Simon—is he human? It was a family joke as to whether there was ice-water or antiseptic fluid in his veins. (Incidentally, with Winston we wondered whether it would be Burgundy or Bollinger '98 vintage.)

One day father came home and announced dramatically that Simon, after all, was an ordinary mortal. Simon had concluded a very brilliant speech in the House that day. L. G. put his hand on Simon's shoulder when he sat down and said, 'That was one of the most telling and brilliant speeches I have heard from anyone. I congratulate you, and I mean it not in any empty form.' Simon turned and (as father described it) almost with emotion in his eyes said, 'George—that is wonderful coming from you. Let's adjourn to the Smoke Room.' On the way father elaborated on his earlier compliment, and they arrived in the Smoke Room full of good fellowship. Simon insisted on celebrating and said, 'Will you leave it to me—we'll have a Bismarck.' L. G. was never a con-noisseur and rather vague as to the contents of the enormous silver jug, pitcher, or whatever the gleaming monster was called; but later he discovered that it contained a small quantity of stout with a full measure of champagne. It looked dark and cool, with just a whimsical head of creamy froth, innocuous in appearance. Father took a sip. Very appetising. It was Bismarck's favourite tipple, Simon said; and they drank to that. Then they toasted the great German Chancellors, their formidable generals, their frauleins, their beer-cellars. Then they toasted Beethoven, Wagner, Bach and Brahms. All was going splendidly until they encountered a difference of opinion as to whether Bach had written twenty-four organ chorales and had twelve children or had twenty-four children and written twelve organ chorales. Father suggested a compromise: he had had eighteen chorales and written eighteen children.

'Well, now,' Simon said, 'that's the sort of remark of yours I take exception to.'

'What's wrong with it?'

'Frivolous,' Simon said. 'It's a frivolous remark.'

'I'll have you know,' L. G. said, 'that a frivolous remark by a remarkable man means a dozen times more than a remarkable remark made by a frivolous man.'

He then read him a lecture about the shape of his head. It was a delectably hilarious interlude, and they both became the greatest of friends—until the magic potion began to wear off. When they rose to go, father said it was as if a curtain had come down over Simon's geniality, and he became again his cold, efficient colleague, the Attorney-General.

'My name is George Nathaniel Curzon,
And I am a Most Superior Person——'

The author of this university jingle was probably the hero of it himself. He was certainly the most witty man in father's circle, and vied with L. G. in the art of the annihilating epigram. About J. T. Davies, of whom he was jealous, Curzon said when father recommended his knighthood, 'It was the most ridiculous elevation of status since Caligula made his horse a Consul'.

He delighted in his own sense of snobbishness. When he achieved ministerial rank, he rang the bell in his office and summoned a secretary. 'Take this away,' he said, pointing to the inkstand. 'The Secretary of State must have silver and crystal, not brass and glass.'

He rather envied father's devastating *mots justes*—of Austen Chamberlain, 'Standing like a stork on the shores of Locarno'. And of Simon, 'He has sat on the fence so long the iron has entered his soul'.

Beneath his façade of pomposity he was a very kind man. Father said to me in a sympathetic moment of discussion, 'He has been trying to live up to his artificial stiffness of carriage ever since, as a child, he has had to wear a metal support for curvature of the spine'. It was a profoundly revealing comment; and from that moment I always discounted the excesses of his snobbishness. A spinal surgeon had been the architect of his mind.

137

At one stage of his career Curzon was summoned to the Palace. Anticipating his appointment as Premier, he was overjoyed. When he learned that the high office was given to someone else, he was so upset that he wept. What a contrast to Rosebery, who accepted the Premiership with a most nonchalant sense of indifference, getting rid of the heavy chore within a year. It was said that he only accepted it because he wanted to fulfil the final boast made at University that he would marry the wealthiest heiress in England, win the Derby and become Prime Minister.

What a gallery! What elegance! The moulds that fashioned them have long since been broken.

Then there was the rugged man from down under, Billy Hughes, a little whiplash of a man with the voice of a bull and a selective deafness. It was said of him that he was too noisy to be ignored, too deaf to hear reason and too small to be hit.

He was a special crony of father's during the wearisome conferences with President Wilson, whose pontifications depressed everybody concerned with them. At one stage, Wilson, adopting his most schoolmasterish manner, asked Billy to make sure that missionaries would be sent to the New Guinea islands recently attached to the Australian possessions. 'Sure, Mr President. The natives have been hungry lately. They could do with a fresh diet of missionary.'

Billy Hughes has always been my favourite outdoor type. He used his deaf aid—a sort of box apparatus—with an artistic skill. When the conversation got particularly dull or pompous he would twiddle the knobs or the wires with a most concerned air, as though the thing had fused.

Mother came in one day, and seeing the apparatus on the table, said, 'Now who's left his camera here?' She whisked it off with the housewifely intent of tidying up—and then, with a little shriek of panic, realised that Billy was attached to the end of it.

There was another Hughes, an American presidential candidate who, but for a tactical campaign error, would have won the election—in which event, there would have been three Welshmen (or men of Welsh origin) represented at the famous international conference after the war. How father regretted that lapse on the part of Mr Hughes! He always maintained that the three of them could have recast world history after the war.

Then there was David's Jonathan—Winston S. Churchill, with whom he was associated longer in office than any other man, and whose personal friendship was the most potent political influence in both their careers; but that story deserves a chapter of its own.

7

WHEN I think of all these brilliant personalities whom I had regarded as the repositories of most worldly wisdom, I am saddened by the realisation that they showed their cleverness in practically all things except the important one. Not one of them seemed to be aware of the thickening darkness of the international scene. They were all, more or less, dedicated to the proposition of Edwardian and early Georgian elegance. Witty table-talk and brilliant repartee, astute debating points on minor issues—it is frightening and incredible to realise that when the first shot was fired that was to echo round the world, no one at home seemed to be aware of what it might mean.

When the news of the Archduke's assassination was reported to the Cabinet, they were thick in argument about the demarcation line of the proposed Northern counties in Ireland. Sir Edward Grey, the Foreign Secretary, made the announcement of the international incident, and then went off on a fishing holiday. No one connected the murder of the Archduke with a plot to force the issue by Germany and her satellites to gain for herself a share of empire loot, additional territories, markets, sources of raw material supply and cheap labour. It was all very obvious from what followed, but no one in authority at home seemed to understand this at the time. They had peopled the elegant set on the stage and formed their artistic tableaux whilst the theatre was being wired by incendiarists.

Winston was more Cassandra-like as a prophet of possible disaster; but his wisdom was mainly after the event. The others had seen nothing of the coming calamity, and did not recognise it even when it stared them in the face.

I feel strongly about this because I was one of a rather large number of interested people—I have fought in two world wars.

I therefore have certain reservations about the impressiveness and brilliance of those in authority.

Father's attitude was confused from the beginning. He had more understanding about political matters than any of them, and far more imagination. From him I had expected some clarifying explanation. There was none.

He remembered very clearly the stand he had taken in the Boer War. Then, he had seen things absolutely in focus. 'Look, here is the meaning to the whole affair—pounds, shillings and pence.'

Germany, the new industrial giant, was challenging us and demanding a share of the possessions we and the French had made our own by exploration and conquest.

That simple issue was clouded in a fervour of sentimental partisanship, artificial loyalties. Suddenly, we were all concerned about the fate of the Serbs or the Belgians as though they were blood brothers. After centuries of oppression and exploitation of the African natives, the Indians, the Dutch settlers, the Irish and Welsh, we were going forth to champion the 'freedom and independence' of the Belgians, whom none of us had cared two jots about in the past, and the Serbs, about whom none of us knew anything at all.

Well, the toast is to our country—may she always be in the right, but right or not—our country! One might argue about the underlying reasons for the war, but one thing is certain: the political leaders should have had some inkling that it was about to take place.

Father's vagueness at the time was due very largely to his loathing of the whole idea of war. Something prevented him from seeing the matter clearly. He was a courageous man, but very normal, and with a great creative urge as a statesman to whom the destructiveness of modern warfare was anathema.

I had often discussed the question of war and peace with him in later years. He was always deeply involved in his conscience about this problem. He certainly did not enter into his rôle as war leader lightly or with the grim enthusiasm which characterised others in the government. He had these attacks of conscience and depression even in the bitterest years of the German war, when he was giving all his strength and mental vigour to the task of fighting it.

In the beginning he was confused and extremely unhappy about the prospect. He even lost his essential grasp of the realistic issues of elementary strategy that were presented immediately by the German threat. Over Belgium, he even said, 'What if we permit Germany just *to pass through* Belgium—persuading the Belgians not to oppose the purely tactical movement? And afterwards, Germany would compensate Belgium for any damage.'

The reader might marvel that a political figure of Lloyd George's calibre would express such a fantastic notion. Apart from the consideration that the guarantee made was in the first place obviously a strategic one, to prevent the outflanking of the French defence by passing through Belgium, the idea of making a deal with a German war machine in full cry was rather like asking a tiger to sign an undertaking not to molest the cattle when he was allowed into the compound.

I quote the following remark to show the extent of wishful thinking that characterised father's attitude just before the war.

'I could never understand—never really believe at the time— that a world war was impossible to avert. The German leaders were civilised, intelligent men. The Kaiser was a devout Christian. As for the idea that they were really concerned with material ends—that they were fighting to gain wealth—I thought of countries like Switzerland and Sweden, who, in spite of their small population or small size, enjoyed a high standard of living. Surely, the pressure was not a material one that could not be solved by the natural industrial genius and hard-working character of the German people.'

This was the gist of father's words—I can at times only quote from memory, of course, although the effect of his arguments was often unforgettable, and my memory was refreshed by hearing him repeat on various occasions similar views.

At the beginning, then, he was very concerned about his participation in any war government. He was thinking quite seriously of resigning and retiring to Criccieth to study, write and practise law—he would not have thrown himself into anti-war campaigning as in his younger days. He had had his fill of martyrdom. He would have followed John Burns, who retired from public life over the war issue, his political integrity finally vindicated, after all, by this sacrificial gesture.

I think that two forces prevailed to persuade Lloyd George to take an active rôle. The first was his secret fear that there was hardly anyone in the Cabinet who would have the imagination and adaptability to steer the country safely through the precipitated crisis; the second was the influence of Winston Churchill, who urged him to throw the full weight of his authority and ability into the conduct of affairs. Winston, as usual, was a lone voice of urgent clarity in the midst of all the dithering. He had mobilised the navy as First Lord, the only arm of the military forces ready for action.

Winston would toss him notes across the Cabinet table, of which this one is probably the most memorable: 'Please God, it is our whole future, as comrades or opponents. The march of events will be dominating.'

Comrade or opponent. That was how Winston saw it, and the plea went home. Father's dream of Criccieth seemed a dusty answer to the problem. He could not sit on the fence whilst the country was in peril. There was this difference with the Boer War —whatever the outcome then, there was no direct threat to the homeland and its people. Now it was different. Lloyd George was not a man to shelter behind Winston Churchill and the navy. The march of events was 'dominating'.

For others, the decision was much easier. For the millions whose sentiments were whipped up easily by catch-phrases, whose imagination was so ineffectual that they were happy to join in a sort of universal jamboree of aggression because it promised a little garish colour and adventure in their lives. 'All over by Christmas!' 'The Russian steam-roller will flatten their tails whilst we give them a bloody nose!' 'Poor little, gallant Belgium! We'll save her from the Hun!' Four weary years of death and hunger and rat-infested mud would shatter their myths of glory; but the millions were ready to fight, ready and willing, long before the man of peace who led them.

STORM LANTERN

1

IN August 1914 war 'broke out'. Many years later, when I asked father to explain how it 'happened', he said to me, 'Well, it happened in two ways—deliberately and accidentally'.

He loved these 'nutty' comments, and I use the word intentionally as a pun. There was sense, sound as a nut, in the apparent contradiction.

The war did not start as a calculated design on the part of an evil aggressor. It did in effect 'break out' rather than start. It was like a germ that spread from the high to the lowly, from small nation to mighty power, from island to continent. First there was a single shot fired by an assassin, and then fifty thousand cannon thundered. Austria marched against Serbia (Serbia? Remember the name?). Russia marched against Austria. Germany marched against Russia. France threatened to march against Germany. Germany marched through Belgium into France. France marched against Germany. We marched. It was like the disintegration of a whole fabric which follows the break of a single chain-stitch.

That was the obvious pattern, but it explained nothing. In effect, it was like trying to explain a brawl in a pub on a Saturday night. Somebody—nobody could remember who—had spilled beer on somebody. There was push for push and shove for shove. Then a bloody nose; then a friend joined in. Soon the whole pub was in an uproar. Why?

Father was firmly of the opinion that it was not a 'capitalist' war, in the sense that the Labour and Socialist pacifists claimed. He described how he had been visited by the Governor of the Bank of England in those early days, who was in a state of alarm. The city was in a panic, he said. A run on the banks was threatened. Shares were tumbling. 'A lot of jelly-bellies,' father described. 'All our hard-headed, "practical" financiers and business men were like a pack of hysterical women in whose midst a rat had been let loose.' As Chancellor of the Exchequer, father met the threat by inaugurating Bank Holidays for Tuesday, Wednesday and Thursday (Monday had been one in the normal course of events)—one of his astute strokes which gave him time to frame legislative measures to restrict the movement of capital, guarantee the stability of currency; it also gave the city time to cool down.

The war started with wholesale retreats on the Western front, and then deadlock in the mud. Britain's 'contemptible' little army —we were a naval power pre-eminently—was forced back in a wide sweep, bundled along by superiority of armament as usual. The generals had learned nothing from the Boer War except how to fight it if it had started all over again. The war soon degenerated to a murky stalemate on the Western Front, and a battle royal at home between Lloyd George and the generals.

'My God, Dick. If they had shown a tenth of the strategy in fighting the war that they did in fighting me and the French General Staff, we could have saved the lives of a million men.' It was the grimmest, truest joke he ever made.

I remember sitting in my dug-out, amidst the muck and desolation, listening to the shells and worrying, worrying endlessly —about the outcome of the battles going on in Whitehall.

Kitchener. What a wonderful poster he made! And later, Haig. 'Brilliant to the top of his army boots,' father said.

Every sensible measure had to be fought for in opposition to the generals. There was the Shell scandal. The shortage of shells made it impossible for us to counter the enemy fire for longer than forty minutes each day. When father tried to induce Kitchener to give army contracts to more firms, he was told that only the 'traditional' firms had the technical know-how to manufacture the weapons. 'They have developed their skill over some two hundred years,' was the proud claim. 'Good God, man!' father thundered. 'They made *pikes* then!'

I have never seen father in more wrathful temper than when he recalled these incidents. 'Kitchener has fallen under the spell of his own poster image. How I curse the day we made a paper idol of that man! He really believes that a war has nothing to do with the government. He thinks that the job of the government is to provide the war. That's all!'

One day father came home and said to mother, 'Maggie, I need three rooms here. I've just been appointed Minister of Munitions. It's a new post, and I've only got a room and a couple of chairs available at the moment.'

He had stepped down voluntarily from the exalted office of Chancellor to the unknown technical job of Munitions (1915) simply because he felt he was needed there. How proud we were of him!

We were later informed that he had exaggerated when he claimed to have two chairs and a table; one of the chairs was taken away because it had been allocated to a different department. The Ministry, launched in this auspicious manner, grew by giant measures almost entirely under his organisational impetus until in its heyday it occupied several hundred rooms at the Metropole Hotel.

Father insisted on building it up entirely in his own way. He scandalised the experienced bureaucrats enlisted to help him in his task by abolishing, first of all, protocol. Anybody with a suggestion could have direct access to him. He was willing to listen once to anybody, and to those who knew what they were talking about any time. He formed an expert team of men from varied walks of life, big business, administration, technical and scientific fields, factory management, social and industrial relations. He organised big meetings at once for business men and factory managers, told them that he wanted to know the capacity of their plants for the multi-purposes of armament production. If they needed money to adapt plant, it would be available. He wanted a minimum figure and a maximum one; he didn't mind how low the first was or how high the second, provided they were accurate.

He was dealing with tough-minded practical characters, men of drive and natural leadership; and he held them all by the force of personality so that they went away like lambs to study the problem. The figures they brought were twice as high as his most optimistic expectation. Everything had been needed: howitzers, grenades, machine-guns, rifles, barbed wire, trenching kit, shells, landmines, lorries.

'How about ambulances?' a voice said.

'We'll send those to the Germans. What we need is weapons,' L. G. joked grimly.

It was a revolution in administration. He had cut right across departmental red tape with a pair of garden shears. Yet he still had to persuade his colleagues in the Cabinet that the production targets must be attained.

Kitchener resisted the assault, not because he could not have used the equipment, but because the pace-maker was a civilian.

'Can you imagine it? A general saying he could not use more equipment? Like a soldier refusing a free —— in a *maison toléré*,' was the memorable remark. Later, he said, 'He resists my proposals like a maiden aunt defending her virginity'.

Kitchener had been asked about machine-guns. 'How many do you need for each battalion?'

'Four. As a maximum.'

The final three words were fatal to Kitchener. Lloyd George thenceforth completely ignored and overrode him. 'When he added that rider, he ceased to exist for me as a serious force in the conduct of affairs,' father said to me later.

Kitchener of course had his friends and supporters in the Cabinet. There was Runciman, President of the Board of Trade, groaning under the example set him by Lloyd George's rocketing passage; there was, in particular, Reginald McKenna, who had stepped temporarily into the former Chancellor's boots at the Exchequer, and found them too big for him by half. It was the temporary nature of his tenure of office that poisoned his relations with father. He had been told that after the war he would have to return the job to Lloyd George. From that time, Lloyd George figured larger as a bogy-man to McKenna than the Kaiser.

Father scoffed at him. 'A ready reckoner. A financier in blinkers,' he described him. He certainly underestimated McKenna's influence, or the influence that his high office carried, because there was difficulty over paying for the enormously increased armament programme launched. The war against the Generals and their supporters was about to commence.

One day father found himself faced with 'experts' sponsored by the Kitchener-McKenna group, who blandly explained why the additional complement of fire-power was not really necessary. The Prime Minister appointed a committee specially to investigate the practical nature of the Minister of Munitions' programme; and this was largely recruited by Kitchener from amongst his subordinates.

They met the Minister and opened the attack. They deluged him with facts and figures about guns, trajectories, saturation fire, personnel, tactics. They proved with scientific precision that the enormous quantity of artillery he had ordered was completely superfluous. Then they withdrew a little in anticipation of the celebrated counter-blast.

But nothing happened. Lloyd George merely grunted.

'Well, gentlemen, is there nothing more you wish to say?' L. G. looked at his watch.

'No, Minister.'

'Very well, then.'

Off they went; and Davies, father's secretary, turned to him in dejection. 'That's a damned shame, sir. I'm sorry.'

'What are you sorry about?'

'Why, our plans. That's the end of the programme.'

'It's the end of the bloody committee,' said father. 'That's the last we'll ever see of that bunch.'

It was; they never met again.

Father went ahead with his programme and, of course, every weapon got full service. He exceeded Kitchener's 'maximum' requirements for machine-guns twice, four times, eight times. By the end of the war a battalion carried a complement of eighty machine-guns, thus exceeding Kitchener's famous 'maximum' twenty times.

The flow of weapons from the factories was a trickle at first. It became a torrent. The rate of increase in production was phenomenal. The difference at the front was seen within a matter of weeks; and it was not long before we were giving the Germans as many bouquets as they had honoured us with. It gave me a marvellous moment of pride when a whole jumping barrage started—origin: our own left flank—followed in a matter of minutes by a staccato clatter—origin: our central entrenchment— and then, from deep in our rear, boom, boom, swish, boom; the heavies at full throttle. I shall never forget the look of delighted surprise on the faces of the men; and one of the battle-stained sweats turned and said to me, 'Eisteddfod?' (Father's favourite musical occasion.)

A wonderful moment for Lloyd George's son.

2

THE deadlock in the mud continued. The German inferiority in mere numbers was compensated for by a compact organisation centrally controlled by the High Command who could, with their interior lines of communication, switch massive troop formations from west to south, from east to north.

'We should win hands down,' I once said to father on leave. 'We have enormous superiority on paper. Why don't we do something about it? There are the Russians, for instance. Surely, if they were equipped, they could swamp the Germans on that vast front, and break the deadlock.'

He struck his forehead with the flat of his hand. 'Never thought of that,' he said benignly. 'Any other suggestions to win the war?'

'Well, hell, what's wrong with the suggestion? We're beginning to turn out the munitions. We could get rifles into the Russians' hands now, surely.'

'The "general" feeling is that we can't.' (He used the word as a pun). 'They're not considered to be trustworthy with equipment.'

I said rather heatedly, in plain soldiering language, that the fighting men respected Russian soldiers and that should be good enough for the brass. As for the Russian generals, history had taught us that they beat a certain not insignificant French general who had wiped his boots on the Prussians. Besides, everyone knew that the Russians were first-class chess players.

Father said that everyone had a theory as to how to win the war. Then he hesitated a while and said, 'Tell me what the great engineer [me] thinks of this. A mobile fort, bristling with guns, that can move along at five miles an hour upwards, maybe, dodge about at the same speed, and to whom barbed wire, ditches, trenches and pill-boxes are not an obstacle. This is top secret,

Dick, so tape up your mouth when you go to bed to be sure not to talk in your sleep.'

I stared. 'A mobile fort like that *could* win the war. Is it real?'

'Well, it's a scheme Winston has been cooking up with some clever technical men. It's a possible.'

'Possible? What a way to talk about a miracle. It's just what's needed to break that stalemate. It's got to be more than possible.'

I discussed this new monster, the superhuman device which would give an extra dimension to warfare, with father on and off all of that leave of mine; and he seemed to be pleased with my response to the idea. He approached it with caution, but I knew that he was quite convinced we had an enormously valuable weapon which could revolutionise the whole conception of warfare. At the end of each discussion father reminded me automatically that this was top secret information, that the very *idea* of the weapon must be guarded with my life, and so on. I got a little tired of his paternal cautions, and pleasantly tried to remind him that I was now old enough to fight for my country and therefore could be expected to keep a secret.

'I know, but don't be tempted to confide in your best friend when he's feeling depressed,' said father, a little sadly, and I knew then how he had succumbed to the temptation to cheer me up a little on my leave. I felt very close to him at that moment.

When I was returning to France, he pressed my hand and said, 'Good luck and God bless. Now don't forget. Keep it tight under that tin hat. If you don't, you needn't be afraid of the Germans. *I'll* personally organise a firing squad in your honour.'

I thumped my head with my knuckle. 'Hear that? From now on, it's solid steel. I can't remember a thing about this leave.'

I felt happy and important and naturally I cherished my secret to the bitter end. (And what a bitter end it was!) Father needn't have worried. The precautions I took might well have amused him. I did not tape up my mouth before going to sleep in the dug-out; but I did seriously and earnestly enquire on my first night back in the line whether anyone had ever heard me talk in my sleep.

As it turned out the precautions and the warnings were all somewhat unnecessary, because the Generals made a present of

154

the idea to the Germans, offering them a number of prototypes of the weapon in the most inept and amateurish manœuvre of the war.

The only satisfaction I had was to be able to say to father, later, 'Any more secret weapons cooking? I hope that there won't be any serious leakage this time and the generals find out about them.'

It was certainly an odd sensation being on the 'inside' and at the front as well. My comrades usually treated me with the friendly leg-pulling all young officers are subjected to, but now and then I could see a thoughtful look on their faces as they regarded me. I remember during one hectic bombardment when we felt very queasy and the shells were beginning to get steadily nearer, churning up the dirt yard by yard towards us, one joker said, 'Well, Dick? Tell us—just between you and us—how's the war going?'

(On such occasions, I always had one answer, 'We're winning.')

This time I made the same answer, but in a different tone of voice—a rising inflexion, which framed the words as a desperately anxious question, 'We're *winning*?!'

One night, although it was relatively quiet, I felt I could not sleep. I lay on my chicken-wire cot, and my thoughts were wandering homewards. I was thinking about father's struggle with those responsible for military operations. I had the greatest respect for his abilities, the warmest appreciation of his single-mindedness and dedication. I was sure that all personal ambitions had been subjugated to the main task of winning the war as far as he was concerned; and yet I thought, 'He's really a weak man. Selfish, self-indulgent—and the lives of all these hundreds of thousands at the front are in his hands.' I felt an extraordinary sense of uneasiness. He was a human being, just as we all were, subject to the same temptations. He was too egotistical. He might overreach himself, and get pushed out by the incompetents who were ganging up against him. Anxiously, I began to compose a speech to him or a letter, warning him against himself, for all our sakes, for Gwilym's and mine—I sat up, lit a torch, and began to scribble a few notes about the points I wished to make.

A voice said, in the dark, 'Make it strong, Dick, and if you like, I'll add a postcript.'

Another voice then said, 'I'll sign it, too.'

Well, the experts on telepathy can make what they want of it.

There was one occasion when I was returning home for a brief leave, thoroughly worn out and despondent by events. A creeping barrage the night before had made me nervous and exhausted. I had not slept for thirty-six hours, and my hands trembled with fatigue. Now and then I felt my heart begin to race as though I had been running. On the train I read one of my perennial favourites, *David Copperfield*, and the sentimental passages made me feel ridiculously close to tears. I seemed to have lost control of my feelings. I was almost at the end of my tether.

'I'll make him understand. I'll *make* him,' I thought. 'I'll tell him to go to the front and *see* what it's like. Why must he be protected? Why should we all baby him?' Sickness, misery, death—these were the only things he feared. He could never look on the face of death. But now he would have to! I'd see to it that he did know what was happening.

When I arrived home I found father at the top of his form, full of bounce and energy. He greeted me with the greatest warmth, and at dinner was obviously trying to make me feel relaxed. He had that wonderful susceptibility to atmosphere which was so valuable to him in judging an audience or during important negotiations. Before the meal was over, I felt certain that without having said a word about it he knew what was in my mind.

After dinner, we were alone, smoking and sipping a whisky. For a long time we were silent. I was trying to find the words which stubbornly refused to come out.

'All right, Dick. You must tell me what it's been like.'

I had had my nose buried in my glass during my agitated period of silence. Now I summoned my resolution. I knew exactly what I wanted to say.

I looked up—and saw a face so drawn and tense and miserable —so utterly different from the cheerful cordiality during dinner that all the words, all the strictures, demands and warnings —they all seemed pointless. Here was a man who had no need to look on the face of it to know death. I had exuded the smell of it from the moment I greeted him. It had hung over me throughout dinner. From the pores of my skin, the roots of my hair, from under my fingernails—wherever I had absorbed it in that nether region—it had been transmitted to him.

I shook my head. Suddenly, I had nothing to say.

Father said to me in a quiet, controlled voice, 'The Germans have recently tried one of their negotiated-peace manœuvres, which was obviously put out for propaganda reasons. They had no wish to have it accepted because they knew that the conditions they demanded would be unacceptable. The only thing to do was to nail the manœuvre for what it was. If the blockade is ended, within a few years they will be three times as strong. Yet to nail their peace offer as a manœuvre was the most difficult, the most bitter thing I ever had to do in my life. I want you to tell me, Dick, not as my son but as a soldier from the front, that I did the right thing.'

Well, I suppose I should have known better than to have planned a debating contest with the old man. He had split my arguments down the middle before I had even opened my mouth.

3

THOSE of us with unforgettable memories of the First World War will remember the first years of it as full of inexplicable muddle, dreariness, inertia and failure. The *Entente* had a tremendous quantitative superiority of resources and manpower, but failed to organise it. There was the failure of the huge armies of the East, through shortage of the most elementary equipment which I constantly 'reminded' Lloyd George about; there was the inexplicable failure to support the Balkan countries, pole-axed by a couple of corps of German troops, switched from the West in a lightning manœuvre of superb timing—thus making available the wheat and oil that the Central Powers lacked. There was the misfiring of the bold and imaginative attempt to seize the Dardanelles through lack of naval co-operation and the most dismal tactical bungling. There was the appropriately named Mespot, with its murderous muddle kept a profound military secret—that is, from the War Cabinet as well as the public. At Jutland we lost more ships and sustained twice the casualties the Germans suffered—although we were left in possession of the ocean, so it was considered a great victory. One of the things Lloyd George was to find in his indefatigable investigation was that at a time we had some seventy divisions in France and overseas, no one had worked out the ordnance requirements of this enormous force of manpower.

The only patches of daylight were in the flow of munitions to the West and the regular feeding of the troops—the Quartermaster-General did a first-class job, as all who served in France will remember. As for armament and equipment, Lloyd George had these organised in terms of production through about fifty regional boards, so that a massive supply was ensured throughout the war.

He had become the outstanding organiser, driver and over-rider in the War Cabinet; and the Prime Minister, Asquith, gave him vast ancillary powers. The Exchequer was virtually a financial adjunct, a secretariat, which he dominated indirectly. Asquith entrusted Lloyd George with every 'trouble spot' problem—industrial friction, Ireland. At this time, as a simple Minister of Munitions, officially concerned with only one purely technical job, he yet carried half a dozen invisible portfolios, to the dismay of the General Staff, the War Office, McKenna and Runciman, who were terrified by his roving commission. He was accused (rightly) of criticising vehemently other departments. 'Wrecking before capture,' was the fearsome phrase used by McKenna.

Kitchener was lost at sea in 1916; and the War Office was given to Lloyd George. Munitions was now a routine matter, relatively speaking, and Lloyd George was confident that he could entrust the continued work of progressively increased production to his lieutenants. The War Office, of course, was the most vital department in the Cabinet, and L. G. accepted the post because it enabled him to deal directly with matters of strategy. He came in head-on collision with the C.I.G.S., Sir William Robertson, and Douglas Haig. L. G.'s plan, even from those early days in the War Office, was to form a unity with allied chiefs of staff and evolve an overall strategy, to subordinate personal and national considerations to the main task of producing an effectively co-ordinated international force, with a central pool of supply, the best military brains to direct operations (irrespective of nationality) and a general reserve that could be drawn on for every weak sector.

He was immediately confronted by personal jealousies of those in authority, national prejudices, the ambitions of small men, lack of imagination, fear of change, archaic manifestations of protocol, bureaucratic stubbornness and the corrosive envy of the incompetent. The Generals were the artificially bolstered idols of the popular Press—an inevitable outcome of war. Their hero-worship by the public was understandable; but what was incomprehensible was that the Press tycoons should fall under the spell of their own publicity campaigns and regard Generals, in face of appalling evidence of muddle and obtuseness, as infallible. In Fleet Street the Generals had their friends, as well as in the departments of Government.

Clémenceau once said that war was far too important a business to be entrusted to the military, and Lloyd George formed that opinion very early in his experience of the 'clique within a clique', that curious cabal characterised by its arrogance and partisanship, the General Staff.

I was once present at a meeting of Haig and my father, and left with a most dismal feeling about the level of intelligence of a soldier to whom our lives were entrusted. Father was trying to explain some particular question about the disposition of reserves, and the arguments were presented from every possible angle to convey comprehension. To say that four times three made twelve would not be enough; one had to add that this was because we had already established that three times four made twelve, too. Haig's part in the conversation consisted of a series of grunts, monosyllables, raised eyebrows and scowls. Perhaps, he was pretending playing 'dumb', but I hardly think so. He would have had to be a clever man to persuade my father that he was stupid when he wasn't.

Father's appointment as War Minister began a phase of his career which established his nickname as the Welsh Wizard or Merlin. It began with a contest of scheming, internal politics, wire-pulling, personal stratagems which would have made him a very worthy subject of study by a modern Machiavelli.

He had always been a subtle man. His skill as a negotiator and committee man was recognised very early during his office at the Board of Trade when he was commissioned to settle important industrial disputes. I have mentioned his sense of 'atmosphere' at a meeting; and he had a wonderful ability to sum up character and personality from early impressions.

In personal contests, he was pretty devastating or utterly unfathomable, just as he chose. He could annihilate with argument or seduce with charm, or out-manœuvre or simply reduce his opponent's resistance by a form of psychological warfare.

As an example of the last, I recall something that happened at a meeting with Kitchener. Father had found it difficult going to out-point Kitchener, who at first was subtle, then supple, then simply unresponsive. There was a bit of stone-walling by both sides, then father turned to Davies, his secretary, and spoke to him in rapid Welsh. Then he jumped up and drawing Edwin Montagu aside, spoke to him rapidly in undertones.

Kitchener raised an agonised hand in protest, 'Good God, the man speaks Yiddish, too!'

There was his hot and cold technique. He could be infinitely patient, amiable and amenable—until his contestant proved intractable to all these affabilities—and then an artificial storm of such terrifying suddenness that his opponent would be reduced to a state of alarm for his personal safety. After his meeting with Clémenceau I once asked him how he had got on with the Tiger.

'Fine. I found out beforehand what sort of man he was. He was supposed to have a very bad temper. Aha! I was in conference with him for about ten minutes when suddenly I appeared to take exception to a minor point of procedure. I jumped up and gave the meeting hell. A perfectly blistering demonstration. Absolute apoplexy. After that, Clémenceau watched me with a wary and anxious eye, I think. He was so worried about annoying me that he sometimes decided to forgo his own annoyances.'

Then there was a 'dumb' technique. He was quite satisfied on occasion to pretend ignorance or obtuseness to drive the opposition through impatience to reveal their hand. There was the time during the meetings in France when he pretended he could not understand French (a language he knew reasonably well) so that he would have time to think whilst pretending to listen to the interpreter. And then (of course) 'you never know what you might pick up from an aside when the parties don't know you can understand them'.

The cunning of the serpent—yes, but the courage of a lion, too. When craft failed, he was capable of taking a calculated risk and driving forward like a bulldozer.

He certainly needed all these skills and all his strength in his contest with the Generals during the years of danger.

'I refused any longer to be a Judas goat leading the lambs to the slaughter,' father said to me once, explaining his decision to get effective control of the war.

Robertson, Haig, McKenna, Runciman, Chamberlain, Cecil,

Long, Curzon, Northcliffe—a formidable phalanx to oppose a man who knew his own mind and believed that the job had to be done his way. Robertson he had tried to out-manœuvre by suggesting that he should go to Russia and study the situation there for a time. The reasons for going were cogent enough; Russia was potentially our greatest ally, the great imponderable; but Robertson was already suspicious of Lloyd George's intentions. Who was to conduct British strategy whilst he was gone? No answer was required. Robertson refused to journey to Russia.

'I did it wrong,' father recollected later. 'I should have pretended that I was going to Russia. Then Robertson would have suspected an outflanker and insisted on going himself.'

The next step was to try to by-pass the General Staff with a special committee, a 'Civilian General Staff', which would include the Prime Minister and three other members, one of whom would be its permanent chairman. Father hoped, of course, that as chairman he would be in effective control, with the Prime Minister generally occupied with the Cabinet or acting as liaison between the Cabinet and the Committee—either way, he would have a merely titular authority.

Father lobbied his friends and allies. Bonar Law looked on him as The Man (Bonar was then in the coalition government and leader of the Tories). Bonar was certain that Lloyd George was the man best able to conduct the war efficiently and effectively. Father had other political allies, of course, but Bonar was the most important—a selfless, highly-respected man. Arthur Henderson, too (Labour representative in the coalition government), was inclined to support L. G.

Then, of course, one had to have a Friend in Fleet Street. That always was the drill. In this case, Max Aitken was a staunch ally.

The memorandum for a new compact war committee was submitted to Prime Minister Asquith, who saw immediately that the proposal to appoint a permanent Chairman of it other than himself would reduce his effective authority in the most important and vital decisions of government at this time. He expressed his appreciation of the necessity to have a smaller

162

and more efficient war committee, but declared that he would have to be its Chairman.

As far as Lloyd George was concerned, that was the end of the war committee. Much as he admired and liked Asquith—and he almost always spoke in the most cordial way about his great gifts —he regarded him as being quite unfitted for the rôle of army bulldozer. Asquith was temperamentally a most gentle and kindly person, and with no sense of the urgency of the vast problems facing the country. Father described him as like a family doctor with a gift for the bedside manner. 'If the patient was making normal progress, he would say, "There you are. You'll be well in no time." And if there was a relapse, he would say, "Now these fluctuations are to be expected, you know. The worst thing is to worry." ' And to worry was just what father thought it necessary to do—even about problems before they arose, in order to prevent them from arising

Lloyd George now saw that with the war committee scheme sunk before it had taken battle station, there now remained only one thing to be done: appoint a new Premier. Bonar Law agreed. He said that Lloyd George would have to be Prime Minister. Father's reply was a very creditable one—and Aitken was present at the meeting to testify to it. 'No, I didn't propose this to become Premier myself. I'll be quite satisfied to act as Chairman of the War Committee. I'd prefer to serve under you.'

In fact, I believe that this was a perfectly genuine expression of feeling. Father's stratagems were not directed towards gaining power for himself for reasons of ambition. It was not ambition that had made him face a war-inflamed populace during the days of the Boer War. He was dedicated to a certain task then, and now there was another momentous one which engaged his spirit to the full. It embarrassed him in a sense, too, for his schemes to be misinterpreted as power manœuvres, as they inevitably were by lesser spirits like McKenna. He was a cynical man—he had had expert masters to teach him the art in his political life—but he was still the crusader and firebrand from Snowdonia, the fighting clansman from the Hills, the orator of Limehouse, the terror of dukes and landlords. He was all these things as well as the expert puppeteer, committee-juggler extraordinary and political chess grandmaster. He now saw himself as the Architect of a Supreme Allied War Council. He was not really interested in the Premier label at the time.

Bonar would not have it. The issue seemed to him perfectly straightforward. The man who was in charge of the conduct of the war had the most important task in the country. It would be an anomaly for such a man to be anything but the Prime Minister.

This exchange of magnanimity between father and Bonar Law, however, did not mean that either of them automatically started packing their personal belongings to move into No. 10, Downing Street. Bonar Law proposed and father finally agreed that he was to be Premier, but there was still the matter of convincing a hostile coalition Cabinet, a bewildered House of Commons and a thoroughly bemused electorate.

This was where Max Aitken was needed.

Father and Bonar Law turned to Max with eloquent enquiry. He responded, 'Leave this to me!'

4

THE stories that broke in the Press were 'sensational' in their implication. A political crisis was challenging Asquith's leadership! If Lloyd George could not get his way, *Reynolds' Newspaper* said (prompted by Aitken), he would resign. He had considerable support. Bonar Law was mentioned; Sir Edward Carson was in sympathy, too, and Lord Derby.

The workings of democracy are often very strange. No one had suspected a crisis until the newspapers started to promote one; and then the fever spread. There *was* a crisis. The conduct of the war *was* most ineffective—come to think of it!

The tom-toms pounding in Fleet Street began to find their rhythms echoing in millions of homes. Lloyd George dissatisfied? The Munitions Miracle Man? Lloyd George resigning? Surely, it must not happen.

The Cabinet was disturbed and incensed. Lloyd George, the schemer, was Trafficking With The Press. 'Wrecking before capture,' hissed McKenna. Lloyd George raised his hands in protest. 'Who—me?' In fact, he had no direct hand in these stories. His 'public relations expert' handled them all.

Members of the Cabinet were highly indignant. A crisis? Not to their knowledge. Most of the ministers were solidly behind Asquith. Lloyd George was alone in this, they claimed. They were completely loyal to the Leader. Put us to the test! Lloyd George will never be able to form a Cabinet, they assured Asquith.

There was, in fact, some truth in this. Lloyd George was far from popular. He was too clever by half. He was a power grabber, a sapper, a bandit. He was no respecter of procedure, of seniority, of tradition. He would drive a coach and four rough-shod through established methods of administration. Mediocrities trembled for their sinecure posts.

But a cold wind was blowing from Fleet Street, and a gale beginning to rise in the country. The Munitions Miracle Man must not go! The boys from the front had told their parents, their brothers, their wives that the flow of arms to the West was almost the only bright spot in the campaign.

Bonar Law was active, too. He wielded a whip over his frightened colleagues in the Tory Party. He threatened to go to the House, to the country, if need be, with Lloyd George.

Asquith could not resist the pressure promoted by the *enfant terrible*, Lloyd George, and his ally, the blunt, forthright Bonar Law. Assured by so many of his ministers that Lloyd George could not form a government—that they would never serve under him—he resigned.

It was a supreme tactical blunder from his point of view, because he commanded loyalty only as a leader. The new leader would be the dispenser of favours from now on (1916), offering plums of office, playing on the susceptibilities of the ambitious, smoothing the anxieties of the timid, giving bland assurances to those who were alarmed by extremes of policy, hotly urging the friends of the former Premier that their loyalty was to their country in times of stress.

L. G. met a deputation of the hostile Tory faction—Curzon, Long, Chamberlain, Cecil—and listened to their 'demands'—that Haig must not go and Churchill (out of favour over the Gallipoli misadventure) must not come in (!). Lloyd George blandly gave them the promise that they wanted to hear. (He later told me that the relief on their faces was 'laughable'.) So now they no longer had reason to oppose him? Yes, that was so. The Tory threat was broken.

The Labour members from whose ranks Lloyd George wanted recruits for certain posts were themselves divided into two factions—pro- and anti-war. He met representatives from both sides, and explained his own attitude to the war. The time for indecision was long past. War was like an illness which demanded immediate action. A week's delay might be fatal. Ramsay Mac-Donald almost alone remained unconvinced but not unimpressed. There was laughter when Lloyd George said that it might be necessary for him to put Ramsay in gaol, but he hoped that on the morning he was released he would have breakfast with him.

By a vote of 17 to 14 the Labour Party decided in favour of alliance with the new Coalition Government, and Arthur Henderson entered the War Cabinet.

There were some who vacillated too long. Edwin Montagu, swearing eternal allegiance to Asquith in the beginning, later phrased this eternal political *cri de cœur*: 'Am I to leave a sinking ship for one that will not float?' He failed to make up his mind between the two alternatives and fell into the water.

Some received more than their due, such as Curzon, who was promoted for tactical reasons to the War Cabinet. (Father was anxious to have a hold on that Tory rebel group.) Others were simply unlucky. Max Aitken had been promised the Board of Trade, a post he was anxious to have in order to exercise his considerable skill and experience in finance, but for a reason I had never been able to ascertain, father baulked at the fence, and Aitken was compensated by his elevation to the peerage. Even the offer of this was framed in a particularly unfortunate way. Bonar Law told him that it was really rather necessary for him to accept the honour because his parliamentary seat was needed for Sir Albert Stanley—whose services were required as President of the Board of Trade!

On more than one occasion I asked father why his trusty old fellow conspirator in the final political tussle was left unrewarded, whilst Curzon—'worth his weight in brass in the War Cabinet'— got such a generous return for so little, but he merely gave me a rather harassed look and changed the subject.

I think that Beaverbrook, as he was of course later known, was one of the few very dominant personalities with whom father was not altogether certain he could work.

I once asked father, during a leisured hour of fanciful conversation, whom he would have had for the ideal Cabinet if he could have had anyone from any walk of life in his (then) rather more than twenty years of public life.

'Chancellor of the Exchequer: Rothschild. Foreign Secretary: Smuts. Labour: Philip Snowden. Colonial Secretary: Billy Hughes. And an Executive Committee with myself as Chairman and two ministers without portfolio, Winston Churchill and Max Beaverbrook.'

I pounced on this. 'But you turned Max down after offering him a job at the Board of Trade'.

He said, impatiently, 'We're discussing ideals now'.

In the final analysis, I had an inkling of what he meant. The three dynamos in an executive committee could have harnessed an avalanche, but they all gave off so many electric sparks that if the currents went the wrong way there was danger of disastrous short-circuits.

The War Cabinet—Lloyd George, Carson, Curzon, Henderson and Bonar Law (Chancellor of the Exchequer and Leader of the House)—had their first meeting, and Carson later said that more was decided in a few hours than in twelve months during Asquith's régime.

The first day of his appointment as Premier father telephoned a shipping magnate, Sir Joseph Maclay, and got him down posthaste from Scotland to organise the production of merchant steamers with Munitions as a model.

The most serious problem was the rate of sinking by U-boats, which threatened to starve us out long before our armies would be defeated. The Germans had about three hundred submarines in commission, and were building them at the rate of more than two hundred a year. The sinister little monsters ruthlessly prowled the shipping lanes, and torpedoed and sank more than half a million tons of our vessels during the worst month of the campaign, topping eight hundred thousand tons of allied shipping.

There were several ways of meeting the continued threat—to arm our merchant fleet, to build more ships, to grow more food, to increase cargo space, to build small naval vessels (camouflaged if possible as merchant ships). These were straightforward, obvious measures that required energetic organisation, and with Lloyd George at the helm, shipping production became a second Munitions miracle. He knew how to pick his pacemakers and executives. Maclay did for shipping what Geddes had done for armaments. During 1917 a million tons of new ships slipped down the launching ramps, a large number of them powerful, compact, even-paced eight-thousand tonners that could outstrip most warships and could carry a pretty useful weight of gunnery.

What of the navy? With the German fleet languishing in the harbours and the German warship production switching largely to submarines, our three thousand major and minor naval vessels were beginning to saunter and 'sit around' like the famous cavalry divisions of General Haig, waiting for the celebrated mythical 'break through'. Wasn't it possible to use the faster vessels of the navy to protect our merchant ships? A stony silence at first greeted Lloyd George's very reasonable question.

Finally, the admirals produced a plan. They suggested that a corridor, or series of corridors, the 'walls' constructed of fast naval vessels, should be formed *at the approaches of home harbours,*★ through which the merchant ships could pass safely to port.

L. G. looked astounded. 'But this,' he stormed, 'would be playing straight into the hands of the U-boats, who would simply gather at the entrance of the "corridors" in wolf-packs to wait for the arrival of the ships.'

The naval strategists looked startled and then despondent.

'However,' L. G. said, 'the idea of a corridor—that might be something. But a corridor that *moves* with the ships, protecting the ships all the way?' And, of course, the 'corridors' *were* mobile ones. 'An escort of naval vessels. A convoy.'

'Now,' the reader might well say, 'a sensible idea. The convoy—I've heard of that, of course. So that's when it all started.'

Well, he would be wrong. That was by no means when it started. The admirals allowed the idea to sink in and then in their turn became apoplectic. What! Make the navy act as wet-nurses for a damned bunch of civilian merchantmen?

Naturally, that was not quite the way they put it. They dressed it with naval science. The merchantmen captains were 'unfamiliar with naval techniques of discipline', would be unable to understand orders, or, if they did, could not be relied on to carry them through. That was the formula. (Really, these were fabulous dodos.)

'Why not understand orders? They spoke English, didn't they? Flag signalling and Morse were common languages at sea, weren't they? The ship's captains had the intelligence to pass Masters' exams, didn't they?'

★ Author's italics.

The admirals retired temporarily behind a protective naval smoke-screen of technicalities; but not for long. Soon they re-appeared in triumph, armed with a favourite weapon, Statistics. More than 2,500 merchant ships *weekly* entered British ports. All the naval forces in the world combined could not escort such a volume of traffic! There it was: a Complete Answer. That would silence the Bounder.

L. G. accepted the figures. He took it all very quietly. A little gesture of resignation. He would bow to the Experts. (He was always at his most dangerous during these moments, as others could have told the admirals.)

They retired complacently to their doodling and dreams of Nelsonian glory.

Then, a shock. One day, into the Admiralty offices entered no less a person than the Prime Minister, brushing aside high-ranking naval officers. He demanded to see the Statisticians forthwith. Before they had the slightest chance to be briefed by their superiors. The men who had worked out the figures of traffic in the home ports. Immediately!

Scandalised by this peremptory rejection of protocol, the broad braid nevertheless could not obstruct the Prime Minister. The junior experts were produced, and they explained that they had computed this phenomenal figure of 2,500 weekly vessels by including every coastal steamer, fishing smack and ferry that knocked about in the harbours and inlets of the British Isles!

The convoy system was adopted.

The success of this mobile protective screen exceeded all Lloyd George's hopes. In the last eighteen months of the war, from a total of nearly 18,000 vessels convoyed, less than one per cent were sunk.

5

THE obstacle to winning the war Lloyd George found it hardest to overcome was General Sir Douglas Haig, who, whilst militarily speaking monumentally stupid, was brilliant in intrigue. He had his friends in Fleet Street, and could match father's Beaverbrook with a Northcliffe. In the country, he was that most legendary of all public idols, the Soldier Hero, and in a straight fight between Lloyd George and General Haig it is doubtful whether the electorate would have plumped for the Civilian Hero in time of war. Father shied at such a contest. Finally, Haig went one better than Lloyd George in his alliances. He established a personal friendship with the King, who had asked him to write to him, saying that his letters would be treated in the strictest confidence. During the most trying of the endless and abortive passages of arms with Lloyd George, Haig was in and out of the Palace like a gossiping housewife torn between two knitting circles. Whilst a corps commander, Haig had jockeyed his chief, General French, out of office mainly through Palace gossip, and became Commander in the Field in his place. Father once said to me, 'We could certainly beat the German generals if only we could get Haig to join them. The German armies would then be a pushover for us—with Haig leading them.'

From the moment he became Premier, Lloyd George was planning to clip Haig's powers—he could not hope to remove him. He tried an 'outflanker', using his 'committee' technique. He persuaded the War Cabinet to approve a scheme to co-ordinate the British and French strategy in the West. General Nivelle was to be in charge of the overall action, and Haig's powers were to be subject to the supreme allied direction of operations by the French general (whom father admired).

Having obtained the agreement of the War Cabinet—no mean achievement with Curzon at the meeting—father then saw Briand, the French Premier, who was delighted with the project. The French General Staff welcomed the scheme and appreciated the honour.

Then father told Robertson and Haig. Presented with this *fait accompli*, the C.I.G.S. and Commander blew up. They considered it a mean trick that they had not been given a chance to solicit their friends in Fleet Street and the Palace. They began to raise difficulties, and father cut them short. He was the supreme constitutional authority; he had the agreement of the War Cabinet for the scheme; and they must know as soldiers the importance of obeying orders in war time. It was as blistering an attack as he had ever launched. He refused to compromise one iota—but knowing the danger of entrusting the lives of British soldiers to disgruntled generals, he cut short the meeting to enable Hankey, the resourceful and flexible Secretary of the Cabinet, to frame a measure that would save face for Haig; if the British Commander thought that Nivelle's action was imperilling our troops he would have the right to appeal to the government. (This would have had the practical effect of merely passing the ball to Lloyd George, of course, but Haig's feelings were somewhat mollified by the illusion that he was able to give them unbridled expression. He did not seem to have been aware—nor had Robertson—that he had that right of appeal in any event.)

The astuteness of Lloyd George's manœuvre lay in his handling of the measure through the War Cabinet in such a way that some of the members failed to see the full implication of it—and of studiously by-passing Robertson, who would normally have been invited to attend the meeting, as it dealt directly with matters which concerned him. But all his subtlety failed to avail him much on this occasion, because there followed one of the most remarkable leakages of information in military history.

A few days before the great Nivelle offensive was planned to be launched, a French N.C.O. was captured by the Germans. For some unfathomable reason he had the Order of Battle for troops north of the Aisne (with all its objectives) in his pocket. How he came to be possessed of this information, and why he should have been captured so conveniently to enable the German Intelligence to have ample time to report on it, has never been established. But to me it seems like the most terrible piece of treachery perpetrated during the war.

The offensive, when it was launched (April, 1917), made some progress at first, but the Germans had withdrawn in all the vulnerable places and left the Western forces punching in a vacuum —and in the meantime they had spread themselves out on open ground, which enabled the German batteries and machine-gunners to deal mercilessly with the attack. The French lost more than a hundred thousand men, and the Nivelle offensive broke down.

All Lloyd George's plans for a joint allied command had to be revised, and in the meantime Haig's star was once more in the ascendant.

For a long time he had been nursing his scheme of a push in the north. In July 1917 he was using all his powers of persuasion to explain how the German front could be broken north-east of Ypres. Within forty-eight hours, Haig argued, he would be through their front lines at certain selected points to enable the 'massed cavalry to pour into the static reserve positions, cut them down and Ride On till they were in sight of the North Sea'. The casualties, he estimated, would be only about 30,000. His G.H.Q. statisticians assured the War Cabinet that our reserves would replace these casualties five times over; that we were, in the absolute sense, twice as strong as the Germans on this part of the front; and that in any case the Germans were becoming so short of manpower that within six months they would come to the end of it.

Haig made no mention of the fact that he had discussed his plan with Pétain and Foch, who were contemptuous of it. 'A duck's march,' was Foch's comment. Pétain was opposed to a large-scale offensive at this time, and all he wanted from the British was that they should take over more of the allied front.

Lloyd George, Milner (War Secretary) and Bonar Law were sceptical of the plan as originally outlined by Haig, but the statisticians' report seemed to support it, and father was desperately anxious to get that cavalry into action at *some* stage of the fighting. Three years had gone by, and they were still kicking their elegant heels, a superbly trained *élite* of soldiers who were desperately resisting 'mechanisation' in the tanks. 'Ye gods—they'll be asking us to be lorry drivers next.'

The Cabinet flashed the green light, and Haig launched his attack.

His choice of terrain and timing was quite remarkable. The salient north-east of Ypres was a former swamp, at that time drained by an elaborate system of ditches that were certain to be smashed by a gun barrage. And he had been told by the meteorologists that the Flanders weather had broken early in August for scores of years with monsoon regularity. So he chose the reclaimed swamp as his battleground, and early August for launching the attack.

Into the slime and runny mud—a sort of curry-yellow, like a vast oleaginous stew—'marched' a million men, carrying their 'indispensible' kit—fighting kit, it was called, weighing close on seventy pounds and including (in early August) rolled greatcoats and hot-water bottles. The men stumbled on duckboards and corduroy tracks which slithered beneath their feet; lines of them in pin-pointed range from batteries of field guns, mortars, machine guns. Periodically, a low-flying aircraft would swoop at what was great speed in those days, and swish straight down the line of men like a guillotine. They stumbled in the quagmire, holding their rifles above their heads, up to their waists, sometimes their necks, for hour on hour in the drenching rain, amidst the grey hell of flying death coming to them in all shapes and sizes, from lozenges to splinters, in the endless jargon of it—the baying of the mortars, the whining of the bullets, the belly-rumbling of the field pieces.

The break-through had been promised the War Cabinet in 'forty-eight hours'. Forty-eight days later there was still no break-through. There was hardly any advance at all. We were not even getting at the enemy, who had watched these flypaper preparations with incredulity and ferocious joy. But there were lies in plenty. We were supposed to have killed Germans by the hundred thousand; our own casualties, on the other hand, were at half that rate. The offensive was going well, claimed the communiqués.

Well? The advance in the mud was proceeding at the rate of a mile a month, and our casualties were twice as heavy as the

German. At this rate of progress it would have taken us sixty years to reach Berlin—that is, provided we could muster an army of about eight million front-line soldiers on that sector in that time.

Haig had his explanation. He had fallen back on his former strategic idea: attrition. The lightning war had not been the success he had hoped, but as we were killing twice as many Germans as they were killing British troops—why, then, the mathematical proof of the success of his offensive was irresistible.

Who was to challenge the truth of a great general's figures? Would the Germans agree to an exchange of teams of chartered accountants?

The newspapers published their 'morale-building' stories with optimistic forecasts of the outcome of the battle. A great communal wave of feverish wishful thinking rose like a spirituous cloud to intoxicate the highest. Lloyd George was fighting almost every member of his Cabinet over his proposal to dismiss Haig and Robertson—without that it would be impossible to stop the holocaust. But the paper idol of Fleet Street was being daily proclaimed a triumphant and victorious general. The whole of Fleet Street could not be fought successfully—even by the British Prime Minister, even when the Prime Minister was Lloyd George.

He said: 'G.H.Q. could not capture Passchendaele Ridge, but it was determined to storm Fleet Street, and here strategy and tactics were superb. The Press Correspondents were completely enveloped, and important publicists and newspaper proprietors in this country were overwhelmed. Lord Northcliffe, ever since 1916, had been the mere kettledrum of Sir Douglas Haig, and the mouth organ of Sir William Robertson.'

> Well might the Dead who struggled in the slime
> Rise and deride this sepulchre of crime,

wrote Siegfried Sassoon in his bitter poem, *On Passing The Menin Gate*.

Whose was the crime? Haig's? Northcliffe's? My father's? 'Here was the world's worst wound.' Who dealt it? The generals who lied, the newspapermen who closed their eyes, or my father, whose nerve failed him in the most important act of his political career?

Who shall absolve the foulness of their fate,
Those doomed, conscripted, unvictorious ones?

Attrition.

'Look—this is Haig's theory,' father once said to me. 'You start off the game with a slight superiority over your opponent. (Imagine a game of draughts.) You have twelve pieces and he has nine. Well, now, you start exchanging pieces, man for man. When you've exchanged three, you're half again as strong as he is—nine to six. When you've exchanged six you're *twice* as strong. You see, that's the theory. It's the Arithmetic of Power. When you have a slight superiority, provided you can exchange man for man, the ratio of strength must grow in your favour.'

I could not look at a draught-board for a very long time after this explanation.

Megan in 1955, when she joined the Labour Party.

Gwilym at the time of his appointment as Minister of Food, 1951.

6

BUT, if father failed to get rid of Haig, he fought and won his battle to get Churchill back in office.

It was an act of friendship.

Politicians are notoriously cynical and 'realistic', and friendships between them are exceedingly rare. I mean, of course, the sort of genuine friendship which withstands success and failure—the other sort breeds like rabbits. Father had dozens of friends in high politics when he was Prime Minister; they might even have equalled his enemies in number. But when he was 'out', it was very different indeed.

Churchill and Lloyd George had been genuine friends from quite early days in their careers. Father was twelve years older than Winston, a substantial but not great age difference in their professional life. Father was a promising younger politician when Winston entered the House. I believe that father cut short his speech on the day that Churchill delivered his maiden speech to allow him more time for it. He spoke later of him as a 'lordly young man, with quite an air—a pugnacious chin and mischievous eyes'. I remember the description, because it is very like the impression I had when I first saw Winston in our home. He was a most handsome young man; and with all the latent strength in him that you felt, he had a great gift of relaxation. He was often gay and amusing, always considerate. His pugnacity was always confined to his political life—unlike father's.

Winston had a very great capacity for the enjoyment of the good things of life, and I won't pretend that he has the reputation of a moral saint, but unlike father he had a sense of personal responsibility to those he cared for and who were dependent on his love.

They took to each other almost immediately, and father spoke of him in a way I have seldom heard him talk of his other colleagues in the House. There was a great deal of admiration for his forcefulness, but a certain impatience, too, and he said caustically one day, 'Winston Churchill mistakes epigrams for policies. Once he's conceived some witticism he proceeds to try to erect a political platform from it.' (This is the gist of it.)

In many ways, both men were remarkably alike. They were both dominant, independent, immensely dangerous in Opposition and capable of daring flights of imagination. Both men had ideals; Winston had scruples, too—father hadn't.

There is a striking similarity in their careers. Winston made such a thumping nuisance of himself (like father) that the government thought it prudent to try to quieten him down by putting him in the team. He followed father as President of the Board of Trade. It must have been galling to an imaginative and energetic young man to follow Lloyd George in office, because by the time father had spring-cleaned the place, turned out all the bed-linen, shaken out the mattresses and done the whole thing over with a fresh coat of glossy paint, there was precious little a newcomer could do except start all over again—and the Board of Trade is hardly a place where two revolutions can be enacted in quick succession. Winston said ruefully, later, 'Lloyd George took all the plums'.

I recall that Winston went off to the Sidney Street 'Siege' when he was Home Secretary, personally to lead the officers of the law and the sappers in their efforts to capture Peter the Painter—just as father went after Jack the Ripper in the very same district of London. (Both quarries got away!)

Both men, of course, became Prime Minister in the very dark days of a world war; and Winston Churchill was able to profit by Lloyd George's earlier experience and activities—a unified Allied Command, the convoy system for merchant shipping, a military attack through Italy, the 'soft under-belly' of the Central Powers —one of father's schemes was to try to get in by the back door through the Balkans and Italy, the front gate being too heavily guarded. These were pages from Lloyd George's book, well thumbed over and studied by Winston Churchill.

Winston was encouraged by the idea of an alliance with Lloyd George to leave the Conservative Party and join the Liberal Party's 'best fighting general'.

They fought in alliance thenceforth for very many years. One of these earlier combinations was an attack on the Naval Estimates, in which Winston assumed the singular rôle of advocating smaller expenditure. The First Lord wanted six dreadnoughts. Winston thought it was too many (!). Father and I had a good laugh recalling that particular episode in Winston's career. 'Had Winston been First Lord he would have demanded sixteen dreadnoughts,' father said.

In 1913 there was the Marconi scandal, which I have already mentioned. This was the most dangerous attack on the personal integrity of Lloyd George in his entire career, and it was a test of the loyalty of his friends that showed their mettle.

It began with the innocent purchase of certain shares in the American Marconi firm at a time when the English company, also bearing the name of Marconi, obtained certain cable and wireless contracts from the Government. Although the English and American companies were quite independent in the sense that the second had no shares or financial interest in the first—and therefore the price of the shares could not be affected by the contract with the Postmaster—the Conservative opposition, together with a certain anti-Semitic faction in the Press, launched attacks on the honesty of the three Ministers concerned, Lloyd George, Rufus Isaacs and the Master of Elibank.

The feats of imagination exercised by their slanderers included the accusation that Lloyd George had profited by some sixty thousand pounds in this deal, that he had properties in the South of France—a luxury villa, yacht and heaven knows what. In fact father's gamble in the Stock Market resulted in a total loss of £200, and the only property he owned was a £2,000 house in Walton Heath—a modest residence indeed for the Chancellor of the Exchequer of the richest country in the world.

'Investigations', enquiries—official and otherwise—dragged on for weeks and months. From first to last the whole sordid business took about a year to run its course, during which all the accusations were dismissed as unproved, and the arch slander-monger, running a scurrilous anti-Jewish rag, was indicted at the Old Bailey for criminal libel. He was convicted, and ordered to pay a fine and an enormous sum in costs.

In spite of this, with all the unconscious cruelty that the human mind is capable of, many well-known and influential members of Parliament in the Conservative Opposition whipped up such a storm of hate against the three Ministers that it had a deadly effect on their nerve. Whilst knowing themselves to be innocent, they became shadows of their former selves. Father was in a state of frightening depression during this period. He would get very absent-minded, and wander away in the middle of a conversation. He would sit and brood for hours. Mother once found him sitting alone in the dark in his room, miserable as a beaten child.

During this time, the man who did most to help, sustain and champion Lloyd George was Winston Churchill. He not only believed Lloyd George was innocent; he was also his friend.

He went to see the most important figure in Fleet Street, Northcliffe, and put the true facts before him. Northcliffe gave instructions to all his newspapers to discount the slanders and rumours of the Marconi affair. 'I am neither a rabid Party man nor an anti-Semite,' Northcliffe told Winston.

Then, during a libel action which the injured Ministers brought against a French newspaper, Winston secured the formidable support of F. E. Smith and Carson, who agreed to appear for the plaintiffs. He had raided the Conservative Opposition alliance to capture their support, a very shrewd tactical move because it also deprived the Opposition of the services of these deadly cross-examiners and advocates.

One of the Committees of 'Enquiry' made the mistake of inviting Winston to appear as a witness in their investigations. He burst in on them with all the cyclonic force of his fighting temperament, thundering, thumping the table and launching such a massive personal offensive that he completely changed the prescribed rôles of the participants in the Enquiry. 'Liars! Cowards!' he roared. The attackers were thrown on the defence, and a very querulous, peevish and ineffectual lot they proved to be.

When the enquiries were over and father and the other two Ministers were finally exonerated, a link of true friendship was forged between Lloyd George and Winston Churchill which was to sustain every pressure in the years to come.

During the war, Winston's reputation dropped badly as a

result of the Gallipoli misadventure. He was Out. For a time he left Parliament and served in France. His stock had fallen so badly that the Tory faction of Cecil, Long, Curzon and Chamberlain made it a condition of their support of Lloyd George's Premiership—they recalled the friendship he had for the discredited man —that he would not invite Winston Churchill into the government. Father needed the Tory support. He was in a weak position —a rift had been created in the Liberal Party by the clash with Asquith. He agreed to the demand. Yet he had not the least intention of keeping his promise to the Tories.

When I reproached him about his promise he flashed at me, 'If I can't convince them, I'll outflank them. If I can't outflank them, I'll smash them.'

At one point it looked as though he would be compelled to take the last course.

He nursed the determination to get Winston back as soon as he was strong enough. A year later (1917), he made the first moves. He was much stronger now. Whilst it would be too much to say that his position was now unassailable—the war had been making little progress in the right direction—it was generally recognised in a sober, rather glum fashion that the man who led the Government was the ablest and strongest person for the heavy burden of that great office. Lloyd George examined the whole position, weighed the facts carefully and came to a decision. He would get Churchill back into effective political life.

He made his first careful reconnaissance. The opposition to Churchill at this time was tremendous. There was a personal element in it, in the sense that it was not activated only by an assessment of the facts about his alleged errors in office. Churchill excited the fears of less talented men. Every strong personality rouses the envy of mediocrities, as father himself had often found, and there is an unnatural relish to which most of us are susceptible when the great ones err or fall from grace. It was these gales which father encountered when he tried to gauge the direction of the wind.

He made enquiries of his colleagues—did they not think that a man of energy and imagination was needed in the government? Was not Churchill wasted outside office? Did he not have great gifts, a fighting temperament, particularly needed in a war leadership?

What—Churchill, that amateur strategist! Bring him back for another Antwerp, another *Dardanelles*! (When it is remembered that Haig, the professional strategist, captured a territory on the Western Front about the size of Kensington Gardens for the cost of four hundred thousand casualties, one might well marvel at the distinction between the amateur and professional in matters of strategy.) But they fastened on the word 'amateur' and made it the pivotal point of every argument. The venom of their denunciations surprised Lloyd George, and would have daunted a less courageous man. 'Some of them felt stronger about Churchill than about the Kaiser,' he told me later.

Apart from the Tory politicians, opposition came from Admiralty quarters. Sir Charles Beresford became very busy organising meetings of protest up and down the country in anticipation of the appointment of Churchill. He also interviewed some important editors. A 'protest' meeting was addressed by the Admiral at the Queen's Hall, where the accusation was made that Churchill had recklessly gambled with the lives of men.

The newspapers gave little support to the suggestion of Churchill back in effective leadership, and one or two actively opposed the idea. Cowdray, of the Air Board, described Churchill as a dangerously ambitious man, and warned father that such a man would claim false credit if the opportunity came and would try to wrest the Premiership from him in time. No doubt he thought that he was dealing with the common currency of power politics. Father had always recognised that Churchill might make a bid for the premiership—it was his temperament. He recognised it, and accepted it. It made no difference to his determination to get him back into a position from which one day he might try to do it. It seems that there are some things that are above power politics, even to politicians.

Curzon expressed concern; Derby, the War Secretary, wanted none of Churchill. Sir George Younger, Chairman of the Conservative Association, and Walter Long, the Colonial Secretary, came out strongly against Churchill. More protest meetings.

Storm signals were now beginning to flash. 'The appointment of Churchill would create a grave situation in the Conservative Party,' he was warned. He was reminded of his promise. Bitterly.

And Bonar Law—Lloyd George's fellow conspirator, devoted ally and friend?

Father had once asked him whether he preferred to have Churchill with him or in opposition, and Bonar had replied, 'In opposition'.

There was a point in these kite-flying manœuvres when Lloyd George stood entirely alone in his campaign. He stood at the summit and looked down from his lonely eminence. Blandishments had failed, arguments had been ineffectual. He was threatened with the desertion of many of his valued supporters, a split in the ranks of the Parties. Never had the appointment of a minister been anticipated with such noisy opposition, such elaborate protestation, so many warnings and threats.

Lloyd George had a remarkable sense of 'atmosphere' in politics. He knew better than most that all his manœuvrings had been in vain, that the image of Churchill in office was a fearsome thing both to the politicians and the Service chiefs. And he was determined to go through with it.

He would make one gesture to placate his friend, Bonar Law—and then, taking a calculated risk, he would turn to face the storm.

Father sent for Beaverbrook, Bonar Law's friend.

Beaverbrook, a power in Fleet Street, certainly had less influence in the field of politics; but he understood Bonar Law thoroughly, and was one of those dynamic few who had no envy of Churchill and no fear of his forceful spirit. He was sympathetic to the appointment of Churchill to the Cabinet.

Father told him that he proposed to make Churchill Minister of Munitions. This was to be an official statement to the Press. But first of all, he wanted Beaverbrook to go to see Bonar Law, tell him the news and reconcile him to the situation.

Thus, with his customary tactical shrewdness, he employed the most sympathetic of all spokesmen to both sides for the delicate business of placating a friend and ally. Beaverbrook spent most of a day trying to mollify Bonar Law, who was angry at first. Finally, however, he was worn down by the persistent proselytising of an accomplished propagandist. (Besides, nobody can stay angry with Beaverbrook. He dismisses such things as irrelevant, and it is impossible to be angry with someone so unresponsive.)

For the second time, therefore, at an important period in father's political career, Beaverbrook was a key figure, an arch ambassador, fellow conspirator or what you prefer to call it—probably all three, in fact.

Whilst the danger from Bonar Law was thus averted, father awaited the main onslaught from the Irreconcilable anti-Churchillians. The anger would come from his colleagues in the government, the House itself and the Press. There was little he could do about the Press, but there was something he could do about his colleagues. He could not any longer entertain any hope of converting them to his view of Churchill. Well, if you can't convince them, confuse them. I think father must have originated that one, too.

As the news swept through Parliament of Churchill's impending appointment as Minister of Munitions, scores of M.P.s gathered in furious conclave. 'Down with Churchill! Down with Lloyd George! Have them both out!' 'He's tricked us!' 'He's broken his promise! Out with Lloyd George and his amateur strategist, Winston Churchill!'

The Tory 'Business' and 'War' Committees endorsed a resolution against Churchill's appointment. The Coalition Liberals had their own reason for detesting the appointment of this ex-Tory who was opposed by his own former colleagues. Letters poured in, all protesting, to the Party headquarters. More than a hundred M.P.s formed an anti-Churchill Coalition Front. Many of them put down questions on the Order Paper.

Some sort of lead was expected from the anti-Churchill Cabinet Ministers. Walter Long wrote a letter to Lloyd George with an implicit threat of resignation. To Bonar Law, he wrote, 'The real effect has been to destroy all confidence in Lloyd George. It is widely held that for purposes of his own, quite apart from the war, he has deceived and "jockeyed" us'. He said that if Churchill tried to interfere with any other department there would be 'serious trouble'.

But where was the organised lead—where the mass resignations? As a bit of diversionary fire, Lloyd George had created a ministerial reshuffle at the time of Churchill's appointment. This shifted the focus of attention slightly, but not enough to divert Ministers with a genuine grievance about broken promises from acting in accordance with their convictions.

There should have been a serious threat to the government, a break-up of the Cabinet, a split in the Coalition. All these had been promised and confidently predicted.

Father's gamble had been made in the full knowledge of this possibility—and the calculated risk had come off. There were no resignations, no schisms, no more threat to the government or the Coalition.

The protests had been a little too loud; the threats a little too bloodcurdling. Father's cynical ear must have detected some cracked note in these outcries. Nobody else did. The appointment was made—and the Government remained. The noisy demonstrations operated in a void of inaction, and soon died a natural and ignominious death.

It was a turning point for Winston Churchill—his re-entry into government (July 1917)—and an opportunity which he fully embraced of proving his calibre as a fighting man in office.

He dined with father at No. 10. After the meal, father took him into another room. There, on a wall, was the framed placard brought out by the *Daily Express* at the time of the Marconi affair. It read, 'Churchill defends Lloyd George'. It must have been a great moment for the two battle-scarred friends.

7

FATHER continued his war against the Generals. The new scheme was to promote a Supreme War Council on the lines originally contemplated, without General Nivelle as Supremo. The purpose now went beyond the original intent of setting up an Allied Strategic Plan. After Haig's terrible blunder in the mud of Passchendaele, father wanted him out of the way, to remove him as an effective menace to the safety of British lives.

He showed me a trick with two hands. He took a coin which he held in his right hand. 'Now, this is the Supreme War Council. Its function is the supreme direction of the allied war effort.'

'What's the coin?'

'That's Haig.'

'If he's in the Supreme War Council, he's subordinate to the Allied Supremo?'

'That's right.'

'And what if he refuses to sit on it?'

'Then it operates without him.' He transferred the coin to the other hand. 'That's operational command in the field. But still subject to strategic control by the Council.'

I shook my head. 'Haig is very crafty about danger to himself. Operational command in the field is all that's needed for effective control.'

Father argued about this, but I remained firm in my opinion. I think I said something on these lines: 'To supervise a commander in the field is back-seat driving. You can own the vehicle and your destination may be the object of the exercise; but you are in the hands of the driver. Haig can find a dozen reasons why his tactics must be obeyed. Finally, he can always say that he alone can see the dangers and the green lights from where he sits.'

Father still saw things 'politically'—that is, in terms of committees. He could juggle with them like pontoon bridges, one over the other—the old bridge was defective so he threw another across the rapids to by-pass it, render it functionless. The by-passing bridge was the new Council, the old was the Haig-Robertson pontoon. But he did not allow for the fact that in the heat of battle you cannot change bridges, and it was the control of battle that was the operative one, no matter what plans were drawn up on paper.

I always thought that the important thing to do was to get Haig off the field.

'Can't you find a way of kicking him upstairs? Can't you fabricate a House of Lords for the military?'

Father still had a faith in the effectiveness of Supreme Strategies. He constantly complained that allied strategy was 'a patchwork' or 'stitching'. He found some response from his French and American colleagues—Russia was out of the war, having suffered about six million casualties as a result of inadequate equipment and official corruption.

By March 1918 we were certainly not as strong as the Central Powers, the Americans had not yet made their massive switch to all-out war effort. It seemed likely that the Germans must stage an all-out offensive before the Americans mustered their full strength. I remember expressing the certainty of this to father, and asking him whether our commanders were really aware of the likelihood and if so what active measures were being taken to counter it.

'They say they are ready. Haig is always ready, he claims.' Then he fell into a deep gloom.

For a time I thought that he was thinking of Haig, but he suddenly came out with it. 'There is an army of about a million and a half men in this country. And I daren't send it to France. I can't take the chance of giving Haig another opportunity to launch an offensive.'

I thought it over for a moment or two and then felt alarmed. 'But what of the chaps in France? And what of the German offensive?'

'Haig tells me that there are adequate forces for any kind of defensive engagement.'

I think this was the bitterest moment in my odd, divided life as soldier and son of so-called Supreme War Leader. Father had just admitted to me his total inadequacy to deal with military events. He had in fact, to my mind, confessed to a bankruptcy of policy. He could neither go back nor forward. The Germans were free to call the tune and he would dance to it.

'We can get the troops out there if they're needed, of course,' he tried to reassure me.

'Yes—when the troops in France are being slaughtered and overrun, you mean.'

'I am told that this cannot happen.'

'By whom? Haig, I suppose.'

'Even Haig can't be wrong about that. Defensive action is not nearly as difficult as offensive. How can he go wrong in matters of elementary tactics? And there is now *co-ordination* with the French and Americans. A general reserve. Everything is ready. All the plans have been worked out to call on reserve for emergency. That is *so*. There has been a general co-ordination of our effort in France.'

Father had become hypnotised by the magical word 'co-ordination'. I think he used it about twenty times during this argument with me, which became very acrimonious.

I thought there was only one way to deal with the situation. Appoint a new Field Commander so that the huge sit-down army in England could be sent out to support their comrades in action.

'You've got to face this showdown with Haig. You've risked dangers before. You risked your life in the Boer War. You can beat Haig in a straight fight. You have to take that risk.'

'What if I lose and Haig remains?'

His words haunted me.

It was a final test for a very great man, and he shirked it.

The Germans launched their offensive in fog—about sixty divisions against our twenty-four on the 21st March. Cooks, sappers, signalmen, clerks took up rifles with the combatant troops to try to hold the solid punch, mounted straight from the shoulder without parley or feint. We reeled back headlong towards the Channel ports. The hinge with the French army was threatened by the direction of the blow.

Ludendorff's plan was to smash that junction of the two armies, sweep us out like an earlier Dunkirk and wheel in round the back of the French defence, enveloping Paris. The offensive ran like a machine. Father would have admired the co-ordination. Peak-fire-power was hit by all weapons in a remarkable synchronisation, like some savage orchestra playing climax music continuously. Forty miles deep bled our wound. It was the greatest British military defeat of the war.

The attack, of course, came as no surprise. Preparations for it could not have been camouflaged by the most skilful machinations, and our low-flying reconnaissance planes had given us ample evidence of troop movements, gun concentrations and every sort of military activity some weeks before it was launched.

Haig fully expected it. He was ready, he said. Our defences were thorough, 'everything' was worked out, and we were secure on every part of the front.

He expressed one anxiety, however. He was afraid that the Germans would find our defences so strong that they would decide, after all, not to launch an attack which would spell such disaster and enormous loss to them.

But they reassured him.

On the third day of the offensive, the Germans advanced deep into our lines in the midst of catastrophe, calamity and confusion. We broke and began to stagger back towards Amiens. A dilemma now, for General Haig and company. Should we try to get out and seek security by way of the Channel ports, or should we try and stay, risking everything ourselves, to help France, who would certainly go down before the butcher's axe if left without our support? Should we retire to our island fortress for another ten-year war, just out of reach of the Teutonic Napoleon?

But what of the Reserve? Where was the emergency force which everybody talked about and which had been conceived with such tortuous scheming? The Reserve Plan which Haig was supposed to have worked out with Pétain was the very hub of the Policy of Co-ordination, Allied Strategy and Supreme War Planning. Haig paid lip service to it. The plans were 'drawn up in combination with the French military authorities and were worked out in great detail to meet the different situations that might arise on different parts of the Allied Front. Measures were taken to ensure the smooth and rapid execution of these plans'.

Lies.

Haig lied, as he lied about the bloody mudbath at Passchendaele, counting non-existent victories, reckoning fictitious enemy losses. Now he lied about Plans of Co-ordination. Even if they had been worked out on paper, there was never the least attempt to ensure their 'smooth and rapid execution' or any intention that they would be. Haig had out-manœuvred father as surely as every German general had out-manœuvred Haig up to this time.

Now, of course, there was a hasty plan to send reinforcements from home. The Germans were playing a full team, whilst ours was at half strength, hanging on the rope with bleeding fingers. Our troops began to arrive in France at the rate of about three thousand a day.

Only one useful result of the débâcle—Haig at last accepted an Allied Generalissimo, Foch. No nonsense this time. No more duplicity, Fleet Street and Palace campaigning, dissembling and histrionics. This was the end of the road for General Haig. Even he realised that he could not survive without expert military guidance. But it had cost the country a million casualties to persuade him.

We made our stand at Amiens, and turned it into another Verdun. The German final onslaught, the great break-through attempt which every amateur strategist knew was a certainty but no professional soldier had properly anticipated, ground to a halt like a locomotive in collision with a troop train.

8

LOOKING back on this personal sketch of the war, I am somewhat surprised and mystified by the end of the story. We won. I remember expressing my thoughts on the matter to father one day when I caught him between Peace Conferences. 'Are you sure it's we who are putting demands to the Germans? Or is it some gigantic international hoax devised by the public-relations boys?'

'It is a little odd,' he said, with a grin. 'But we did win in the end.'

'How? When we were losing all the way—Gallipoli, Mesopotamia, the Somme, Ypres, Caporetto, Tannenburg.' I started listing the Allied defeats on my fingers. Father cut me short.

'We won on three counts. Our naval blockade. French generalship.'

'And the third?'

'The German blunder of getting the Americans into the war by sinking their merchant ships.'

'Now why should brilliant strategists like the Germans make a blunder like that?'

'They thought they could starve us into submission through their U-boat campaign before the Americans had switched to effective participation in the war.'

'So it was your convoy system idea that really beat them?'

'Now,' father said in his mock-modest manner, 'you said that. I didn't.' He laughed. 'I'll tell you who really won the war, Dick. You did. The chap in the steel helmet.'

And he dashed off to another Conference.

The end of the war did come as a vast surprise to many fighting men. A few months ago we had known a defeat of such magnitude that it seemed touch and go. Then, in the summer of 1918, with Foch effectively co-ordinating French and British strategy, the tide began to turn. We were pushing steadily forward on the crest of a continuous barrage, preceded by squadrons of tanks, used in mass at last, as the back-room boys had originally envisaged their purpose. We were not making sensational breaks in the German lines, but we felt our punches beginning to tell even against the muscle-padded bulk of our monumental foe. Even so, he was retiring in good order, with plenty of fighting heart, and the ropes seemed far, far away.

Then, one grey, sombre autumn day, the news began to flash through the soldier grapevine. 'They're cracking. They're ready to cry off. It's true. *Can* it be true?'

It was. Suddenly, it was all over. The Germans were ready to sue for Armistice. Unbelievable, but true.

There was plenty of fight left in them yet. We all knew it. The German High Command were gloomily but painstakingly filling in the details of a winter campaign. The German factories were studying blueprints for the mass production of six thousand special anti-tank weapons. But someone—some German professor of statistical techniques—had worked out that the ratio of strength was remorselessly rising against them, and the statesmen knew that they could get a better bargain in peace negotiations with foreign troops outside German soil. So they switched the object of the exercise from winning the war to winning the peace. They dismissed their soldiers and recruited their loudest and most talented cry-babies to attend the Peace Conference. 'We have given up our weapons. But our women are hungry. Our children are dying from starvation. They are the innocents. For mercy's sake, ease the blockade.'

Father's sensitive heart could not fail to respond to such a plea.

The French were cynical. 'Starving German babies? Well, what of it? Today's German baby is tomorrow's goose-stepping Prussian trooper.'

The American President Wilson was proof against any sort of argument which did not fit into the moral framework of his Fourteen Points.

Orlando, the Italian, was hardly listened to in the debate.

The demands came: reparations, colonies, Alsace and Lorraine, the German navy, strategic bases.

(*Above*) My father and Frances Stevenson on their wedding day.

(*Below*) With some of the land-girls from the farm at Churt, on his 80th birthday.

My mother.

The Powers argued and harangued round the Conference Table.

The chief cry was for reparations, to squeeze the German lemon till the pips squeaked. But how could they pay? They were an impoverished nation. They had little gold. If they were to pay with goods, this would constitute a threat to home industries! The victors were defeated before the peace offensive was launched.

Father's concern was to abolish the premises of a future war. Never mind about personal vendetta. He worked with all his energy—to me, it came to seem obsessional—to establish an unbreakable chain of interdependent treaties, compacts, alliances, non-aggression pacts. He still believed in plans on paper, co-ordination—this time in the realm of world politics. It was a staggeringly ambitious project. In the years immediately following the war there were thirty-three international conferences, sometimes with ninety or more nations represented. The map of Europe was being re-drafted with as much intellectual battle heat as had been formerly shown in the realm of military engagements—except that this time the war was going on chiefly amongst the former allies. Wilson had the reputation of being the Moralist, but Lloyd George became known as the Prime Minister of Europe, and acted as a buffer successfully between the aggressive French representatives and their American and Continental allies. In the final analysis, a general settlement produced a new European continent whose nations occupied their own countries —a remarkable outcome in view of the mass expression of bitterness between the victorious and the defeated. This was Lloyd George's aim, directed at abolishing ready-made excuses for future aggression.

No one, of course, could have anticipated every form of excuse for would-be aggressors—particularly as in many cases none is needed—but the effort was made to restrict them and to make international law-breaking more evident.

I am conscious that father was rather carried away by his idealism in these giant purposes. Of the thirty-three conferences (during which millions of words were spoken by hundreds of delegates, and the result of which was a whole paper-chain of agreements to circle the globe), which of them are anything but torn scraps of paper today? Which, if any, of the millions of words, are remembered today? What of Wilson's League of Nations—rejected by the country which originated the scheme? And how many of the redrawn boundaries of nations survive today?

It is a sad comment on idealism that the only known method of abolishing war is to make it impossible to be waged success-fully—to produce weapons of such horror that they alone can ensure peace. And such weapons had not been invented in Lloyd George's time.

Thinking back, all I can remember about these years of debate and argument in the greatest forums of mankind's history are a few personal comments father made about his opposite numbers. He was a little caustic about Wilson—Clémenceau, I believe, said that the good God was satisfied with Ten Points but Wilson insisted on Fourteen. And another French representative remarked of Wilson that he talked like Christ but behaved like Lloyd George!

And I remember father's description of the golf game that brought down the French Government.

This was at Cannes.

Father, as I have recalled, used golf less as a recreation than a form of mental aid (like Winston's brick-laying)—his golf games were almost invariably occasions for the deeper discussion in private of particularly important matters. At Cannes he had some important things to talk over with Briand and the Italian representative, Bonomi. He offered to introduce them to the game of golf. The three of them turned up on the course. Briand was delighted with the wide range of clubs, which he regarded as weapons with which to express his inhibited aggressions. Bonomi, too, ignored all instruction in the contemplation of this arsenal of metal-headed well-weighted clubs. The little white ball served as a target quite successfully—but not to be manœuvred on to the green or into a hole. They wanted to see who could hit it the hardest. In spite of father's amused protests, the excited French-man and carefree Italian made the most extravagant demonstra-tions—delighted when they sent the ball over the horizon, and furious when they sent up vast clods of earth.

After a while they were prevailed on to try to 'pot' the ball. Then, with exaggerated exhibitions of finesse—crouching on all-fours, sighting the ball like Lindrum about to make some spectacular oblique multiple-stroke—they tried to lure the ball to its destination, coaxing, cajoling, pleading with it on bended knees, reviling and abusing it—and when, after many vain efforts, succeeding in holing it, receiving the rapturous congratulations and warm handshakes of their Continental colleagues.

It was all rather good fun, and an excellent safety-valve for the tensions of committee work, but the pictures published in the Continental papers the following day were received in France with a storm of indignation that the French Premier should have made such a spectacle of himself—and so obviously been made a public fool of by the wily duplicit British Premier, Lloyd George.

Briand thought it necessary to return to Paris and placate the Assembly. He never returned to Cannes. The French Government collapsed as a result of his first lesson in golf from Lloyd George. Which turns out to be rather a sad little story, after all; but sadder still it is to think that that is probably all that history will remember of that particular conference.

Whilst father was so busy with these conferences (1919–22), there was trouble at home and abroad. Winston was trying to promote anti-Soviet military expeditions. We had accumulated stocks of equipment for our former Russian ally at various ports, and in order to safeguard them now that they were liable to fall into Bolshevik hands, small forces had been landed by us. Winston wanted to make these police detachments spearheads to launch offensives against Communist Russia.

Lloyd George was, in general, very much in opposition to these enterprises. 'Nobody can defeat Russia on Russian soil,' he once said to me. 'It's like trying to fight the ocean. Napoleon found that after a dozen victories all that he ever captured was the ground his troops stood on.'

Of Winston's anti-Soviet schemes, he said that the Churchillian ducal blood was feverish as a result of the death of so many archdukes, and Winston could not be relied on to think clearly on that particular matter.

Father usually had his tongue in his cheek when he conformed to the pattern of denunciation of Sovietism. He had a sneaking sympathy for the Radical experiment, irrespective of its form. He deplored tyranny, but he had no horror of outraged landlordism and corrupt aristocratic rule. He regretted that he never met Lenin. Lenin and Mussolini were the only two outstanding political leaders of his time with whom Lloyd George did not make personal contact. (Mussolini, as a journalist, once tried to interview him, but father was too busy to see him!)

9

THE only really important effect of the interminable international conferences was that Lloyd George lost contact with home affairs. It was vastly regrettable. He became so obsessed by foreign-policy matters that he overlooked the great changes taking place in the political climate at home—particularly a swing to the Left, which recast the whole character of Parliament in future.

Father was a good Radical Liberal, probably further to the Left than most Labour members of Parliament—in practice, where it counts, that is. Many of them made protestations about the necessity for sweeping changes and vast reforms when Labour was in opposition. In office, they were almost all hopelessly inept in conceiving workable schemes, and lost every opportunity of taking any sort of effective action—and I bear in mind that they did not often have clear majorities except in coalition. But father produced some of his most daring and telling measures in no more favourable circumstances—by mastering his text, personal magnetism in committee and dominance in the House. The great social insurance schemes, the industrial reforms, the reforms in the Lords—all these were launched in the face of bitter opposition and great prejudice. His anti-war campaign was conducted at great personal danger.

Politically speaking, he was still a young man—fifty-eight—when the great challenge from the Left helped to diminish the Liberal ranks.

The soldiers returning home from the Front, the newly enfranchised women—factory workers in wartime industry by the million—were in no mood to tolerate unemployment, poverty, exploitation. They had been promised a land fit for heroes. Their leaders were susceptible to the popular representation of Socialist doctrine by the great literary propagandists of their time—where are they now?—the Shaws and Wellses, the Russells and Webbs. Soviet Russia was a challenge to direct action for many intelligent leaders of working-class organisations faced with rising unemployment and cruel hardship. The workers were getting a raw deal, conscious of war profiteers in their midst. The dockers refused to load the munitions for ships destined for anti-Soviet expeditions.

These were the danger signs, the warnings of brittleness of public temper; and Lloyd George, who had always been so sensitive to political temperature, would not have failed to adapt himself to it in former times.

Now he was something of an international legend, a pedestal figure—conscious of his rôle as Prime Minister of Europe, of his assured place in history; too conscious. He scored his empty successes at the international forums—and he missed the doorstep on his front porch.

There was a final act of statesmanship, a last far-reaching measure to prove that the hand still retained its singular cunning and the brain its genius for subtlety: Ireland, the problem that had defeated the Strongbows and Cromwells and Gladstones. To my mind, any man who could solve the quandary of Ireland could solve anything in politics. Lloyd George finally found a formula for Ireland which bears its imprint to this day.

Ireland was always a remarkable problem in that the Irish themselves could never agree as to what it was. Independence, partition, Home Rule, Dominion status, republicanism—nobody knew what the Irish leaders wanted, least of all themselves. It was a problem that was continually being examined—and inevitably shelved, till the next outbreak of violence.

There were the Irish who were anti-British, the Irish who were anti-Capitalist, the Irish who were anti-Protestant, the Irish who were anti-Catholic, the Irish who were anti-Unionist, the Irish who were anti-Irish. Yes, there were even some in the last category, in the sense that they were violently opposed to rule by their own nationals and any sort of break with Britain. They feared to sever ties with a rich, powerful, highly industrialised, modern state in which there was abundant opportunity, relatively speaking, for personal development.

The dilemma of Ireland was not a joke, in spite of the comic-opera element about some of the personalities who featured in its resolution. We in France fought side by side with famous loyal Irish regiments, whilst at home, in Dublin, their brothers or friends took part in the savage, ill-fated Easter uprising—that vicious kidney punch to the turned back of the ancient English foe.

Did the people of Ireland want complete severance from the British Empire? Did they really want to cut themselves off from the wealth and personal opportunity that membership of this power-ful group of communities offered them? Father had been a fight-ing 'nationalist' in his day, but even in his most turbulent period as a Welsh clansman he was only after Home Rule, with Dominion Status as a cautious proviso—so that whilst he shouted his battle-cry of Independence he wanted a key to slip into the back door of the manse where the big table was well laden with the rich provender. And when he recognised the ambiguity of such a rôle in the small compact island community, he hastily dropped Home Rule from his political programme.

The Irish fought their way to independence for the twenty-six Southern Counties—but, after all the bloodshed, all the fratricide and martyrdom, have the people really got what they want? A poor, agricultural community; the worst censorship of any English-speaking nation; mass annual emigrations which leaves the country peopled mainly with the old and the very young. And Dublin is the only city in the English-speaking communities where barefooted beggar children prowl the main streets and highways. As for Home Rule—what government façade effec-tively conceals the hidden hand of the Vatican?

I had often discussed Ireland with father, who frequently maintained that the people of Ireland knew as little as did their 'leaders' about the consequence of Independence.

The 'leaders' were a queer, gallant, proud, mad collection of gangsters, poets, patriots, bigots, adventurers, opportunists, political schemers—a colourful crew. They became a dangerous nuisance during L. G.'s premiership, provoking violence, in-viting savage reprisals from the hand-picked special constabulary, the Black and Tans. Amongst their number were men of noble conviction—Terence MacSwiney, who went on hunger strike for seventy-four days in Brixton Prison, committing suicide in protest against 'tyranny'; men of courage and obstinacy, such as De Valera, who offered his life to the firing-squad commandant to free the ringleaders of the Post Office uprising; men of wit and gallantry, such as Michael Collins, the 'Big Fellow', Director of the underground army, who broke every rule of concealment by openly going about without any sort of disguise when there was a price of ten thousand pounds on his head.

'There is an army of a hundred thousand opposing us,' Lord French said.

Fear has big eyes. Michael Collins claimed that his forces numbered less than four thousand men; and there were probably no more than ten thousand. Yet they gave as much trouble as a German army corps, and gave rise to more anxiety. There were the mass assassinations engineered by gangs of tough youngsters —on one occasion they broke into the homes of British officers and shot them down before the eyes of their horrified wives and children. This beastliness was matched by the behaviour of the Black and Tans, who set fire to buildings and prevented the fire brigade from putting them out by slashing their hoses; who shot up a crowd at a sports meeting, killing and injuring innocent spectators who had nothing to do with the warring factions.

These terror campaigns had to cease; and Lloyd George refused to listen to die-hard colleagues demanding complete military occupation of Ireland. He wanted to negotiate. He wanted a meeting with the Irish leaders to thrash out their differences.

De Valera was the obvious man to attend such a meeting; but he had a curious, obstinate, oblique technique in dealing with invitations to have it out with Lloyd George. I am sure he was afraid of father's reputation in committee, his wiliness as a negotiator. After innumerable exchanges of letters and telegrams he did attend such a meeting which seemed to go on for ever.

After it was over, I eagerly asked father what progress had been made. 'Well, we've covered about three hundred years so far. We've reached Cromwell.'

He described the meeting as a merry-go-round, with De Valera mounted on the wooden horse just ahead, bobbing up and down and always just out of reach.

Father had known a few stone-wallers in his time—he was a master of this technique himself—but no one to compare with the dour Spanish-American, appointed by the dedicated republicans to lead the Irish.

Father was sick of the Irish republicans. He was quite willing to let them have independence to go their own way and become what they seemed determined to become, an impoverished semi-peasant community with their peat fires and undrained bogs and dreams of glory seen in a fine mist of alcohol. But there were two things he demanded as necessary provisos—the Irish who wished to retain British citizenship (as so many of them still wanted to do in the North-east Counties) would not be sacrificed to appease the republicans and he wanted to ensure that the Irish ports and harbours—the strategic bases required for the safety of the United Kingdom—would be controlled by us.

He was willing to make some sort of concession on the second point—the overwhelming military and naval powers of England could ensure control of these harbours in time of war if this really became necessary. But on the first point he was, at first, quite adamant. He would not create a minority within a minority. But the Irish, so passionately concerned about their own fight against the tyrannical overlordship of Britain, insisted on exercising it over that part of their community which still insisted on union with Britain. And they used exactly the same arguments as the hated die-hard overlords—it would unbalance national economy, break their 'cultural' pattern, divide 'brother from brother'. This yearning for racial integrity did not extend to the man they chose to be their leader, the American of Spanish extraction, who had not even bothered to 'racialise' his foreign-sounding name.

Father used all his skill in debate to seek to persuade De Valera that 'unity' with the non-nationalistic elements would be abusing the very principle of self-determination which De Valera was advocating; but the 'Irish' leader or non-Irish leader of Irishmen insisted on using the sort of logic popularly attributed to his 'countrymen'.

In fact, De Valera could not, with personal safety, make this concession. He would be shot by his own colleagues as a traitor if he accepted 'partition'. I think this was the reason for the enormous reluctance he had shown in accepting father's invitation to negotiate; and it certainly explained his stone-walling.

This stone-walling was resumed by another Irish delegation later, led by Arthur Griffith and Michael Collins, who had been instructed by their 'government' to sign nothing, but report back to Dublin.

They talked all round the subject—the oath of allegiance, Dominion status, a boundary commission to define the border States, a separate Irish Parliament for Ulster and the possibility of making this subordinate to the Southern Parliament. Lloyd George had decided on a waiting game, to make no concessions of any kind until the delegates showed sign of strain. He was then prepared for a concession on the parliamentary status of Ulster provided the delegates would concede on the oath of allegiance to ensure safety of strategic ports and harbours.

After innumerable meetings, when the nerves of the contestants were strained to the limit, Lloyd George made his conditional concession—and it was accepted by Arthur Griffith.

He was prepared to concede the issue of self-determination for both 'Irelands'—the Free State and Ulster—which might technically give some semblance of dominance to the South, provided a formula would be accepted to ensure the strategic association of Ireland with Britain through a technical oath of allegiance.

This was not really satisfactory to either side—there would be explosions from the 'Irish Free State' government, and the people of Ulster would feel they had been let down by their champions; but in the circumstances no solution acceptable to both sides was possible. Father simply wanted a Treaty. He wanted the agreement to stop the fighting.

Once a Treaty of some kind was signed, a new element would enter into the situation—the will to war would be undermined. This was his object. He was fully aware that the fighting was only possible by a tremendous act of dedication, and this he was determined to sabotage. The Irish did not want to live in a state of underground siege permanently with the British. Whether the Treaty was an empty formula or not, it was an indication to the rank and file of Sinn Fein that their leaders were not fanatically bent on uncompromising war to the finish. And it would be enough.

It was a long time before the other delegates were persuaded to consider the 'formula' even as a possible solution. Lloyd George left the conference room after a while to let them wear each other out with empty argument and wrangling. About an hour later, with no decision reached and a sullen silence prevailing, he returned with a look of purpose.

'I have no time left. Is it to be agreement or war?' He held up a letter. 'This is going to Sir James Craig tonight. You gentlemen must decide whether there shall be peace between us—or whether it is to be all-out war to the finish! The skirmishing is at an end.'

This was the sort of move that De Valera had instinctively feared—the unexpected body blow, a demand for a decision where none was possible.

L. G.'s weeks of negotiation had had just that purpose—to wear down the resistance of the Irish delegates to the point where they were at the very lowest ebb of resolution—and then deliver the most powerful punch. It was cruel and hard; and the delegates who signed the Treaty of December 1921 had the pallor of men who were signing their own death warrants. As, indeed, was true in the case of Michael Collins, who was shot.

But the rattle of machine-gun fire in the streets died down.

WILDERNESS

1

FOR some time I had been noticing father beginning to change. A man who had served for six years as his country's Prime Minister, who had become known in turn as The Man Who Won The War and The Prime Minister of Europe, could not (understandably) remain unaffected by the adulation he had come to regard as his proper due. Women continued to flatter him. I suppose he would have had to be superhuman not to become intoxicated by so many honours, so much idolatry. He had behaved for a long time with a prima-donna-like temperament, but this, in a way, was something of a joke. His secretaries and assistants were only too willing to show their devotion, and to cater for his idiosyncrasies and capricious moods was to render proof of it. There was not another man in public life who could have got away with the lack of consideration to subordinates that he showed; but they ran round him in small circles, fussing over him and letting him treat them as a doormat.

He was never an unkind man; nor cold; nor fond of cruelty for its own sake; but gradually he had suffered a metamorphosis of personality, beginning to take for granted his infallibility, supremacy. He was beginning to believe implicitly in his permanently ascendant star.

Women played a too-active part in all this. He had a reputation for susceptibility that never let him down. A good-looking woman was not necessarily the only one assured of victory. There was a whole wide range of qualities that appealed to him. The 'quiet' type. The 'deep' type. A woman needed to have no obvious attractiveness to appeal to father. He usually succeeded in finding something 'interesting' in almost any female with whom he was more than casually associated. And they made it very easy for him, generally speaking; their egos were excited by the prospect of the conquest of Britain's Prime Minister.

All these private amusements took up a not inconsiderable time, let alone energy; and something had to be neglected.

It had to be the House of Commons.

For weeks, months at a time, he did not set foot in the House—he who at one time practically lived in it.

I remember a cartoon in *Punch* depicting father and Bonar Law on Westminster Bridge. Bonar flourishes his umbrella in the direction of the Houses of Parliament and the caption reads, 'Come and have a look at the old place once more. I think I could get you in'.

I had a twinge when I saw it, an uneasy feeling, and my memory went back to the days of his stormy, enthusiastic youth when he had not been too busy, even for his law practice, to attend every important session, every notable debate.

I was buttonholed one day by a hurrying figure just as I was about to go to father's study. 'The Government has just been defeated!' I was told.

'Defeated?'

'Yes. Not an important issue. And it does not mean that the Government has fallen. But there was no leadership in the House, and no one had expected a division. I—was wondering—would *you* tell Mr Lloyd George?'

My informant was undoubtedly nervous of the old man's reaction, so I went in to tell father myself. I found him—rather uncharacteristically, with a glass of brandy in his hand; and a rather flushed youngish woman was hastily retiring from him.

I did not apologise for disturbing him.

'What do you want, Dick? Why don't you knock?'

'Never mind about that,' I said, roughly. 'The Government has just been defeated. I thought you would want to know.'

'Defeated? Impossible!' He sat up in such indignation that I started to laugh. 'You're joking,' he said, angrily.

'How would you know whether I'm joking? When were you last in the House?'

I went out rather stormily, and I think I shut the door somewhat loudly.

It gave him a minor jolt; but he soon began to slip back into his former habits.

A particular lady friend of his was Frances Stevenson, who had been interviewed by him originally to coach Megan in preparation for a boarding school. Frances Stevenson was a teacher at Wimbledon Girls' School, a young woman of twenty-three at the time. He engaged her to help his daughter in her studies. The appointment was originally intended for a few months, but she stayed permanently.

Frances Stevenson was a quiet, self-contained young person, but she had her moments of eloquence. She found Lloyd George remarkably attractive.

I quote from her description of him: 'I recall—the sensitive face, with deep furrows between the eyes; the eyes themselves, in which was all knowledge of human nature, grave and gay almost simultaneously; eyes which, when they scrutinised yours, convinced you that they understood all the workings of your heart and mind, sympathised with all your difficulties, set you in a place apart. The broad brow; the beautiful profile—straight nose, neat insolent chin. And a complexion as young and as fresh as a child's. But there was something more even than this which distinguished him from all other men I had ever met—from all men whom I ever did meet thereafter—a magnetism which made my heart leap and swept aside my judgment.'

This young lady with the magnetised heart and disturbed judgment became a permanent fixture in our home. She was appointed father's secretary.

In the years immediately following the war, I had the nerve to try to tackle him about his way of life. I had been through tough times, and did not mind very much about a certain roughness of speech which he was hardly accustomed to from me or anyone else. I was distressed to feel that he was slipping away from everything important to him. He had hurt mother repeatedly and needlessly; and she gave him the stability that was vital to him.

'This is just as important to you as it is to mother,' I told him. 'Why don't you straighten things out? Clear the decks. You're surrounded by false friends who are using you and building you up to a God-almighty fall.'

He became very angry, and we parted with a certain bitterness at the time.

I know it is difficult for a son to justify criticism of his father; but I had been through a war, I was sick of seeing people hurt, I was afraid for his future without mother's loving influence, and I was distressed by the endless hurts he had inflicted on her when these women really meant nothing at all to him except some titillation of superficial desire. I had watched him turn to sycophants, fools, flatterers, scheming women, so that important affairs began to get out of focus.

There was bitter industrial unrest, an urgent need for statesmanship, problems which in the old days he would have tackled conscientiously. If only he had turned his giant organising energies to the business of nursing our national economy to health after the cruel devastation of war, instead of allowing them to begin to slip in a flaccid grip!

There was literally no one else. Bonar Law lacked the imagination; Churchill lacked the contact with the common man; Asquith was becoming a dodo; and the Labour men had neither the drive, resourcefulness or know-how to make any impression on events.

Father had left himself little enough time to deal with home problems in his endless foreign trips. He needed every hour God made to stem the drift towards industrial anarchy—all his wits, adaptability and energy.

He could have done it. He had the gifts and the immense experience to tackle the problem and beat it. And he could have carried the country with him—whatever revolutionary change was necessary. Everyone believed in him. He had had the people on his side—the workpeople, whom he had championed in his Soak The Rich Budget. He had emancipated the women. Even the city had regarded him as a hero since he had averted the financial panic in the days immediately following the war. The big-business executives respected him tremendously; they did not forget the organisational miracles he had performed in Munitions and Shipping.

It was all in his hands. A bold, imaginative and workable economic policy—and he could have gone to the country for all the support he needed.

His mind was on other things.

And then he perpetrated an act of incredible folly.

On the face of it, it was the most remarkable piece of financial sleight-of-hand ever executed—because he disregarded ethical considerations and outflanked the legal system. In a sense, it was the smartest piece of strategy ever devised by the Welsh Wizard. And yet it was also inconceivably stupid—and totally unnecessary.

2

AFTER the war, Haig became an earl and was given a grant of a hundred thousand pounds and an ancestral mansion. Every Tom, Dick and Harry in the war leadership was showered with honours and favours. The exception to this was Sir John Cowan, the Quartermaster-General.

Now those of us who served in France had the warmest memory of this fine and conscientious man. Whatever the situation, however tough the going—even when we were up to our elbows in mud—the rations were served to us on time. In the midst of devastation, amidst blizzards of flying shrapnel, the 'grub' was delivered. Whatever else, the army was well fed. They were good rations and plentiful. If ever a man deserved an 'honour' it was Cowan.

I said to father, 'What are you recommending for Sir John? A full peerage, I hope.'

Father shook his head. 'Most distressing. I have spoken to H.M.—but Cowan was indiscreet. A certain titled lady. H.M. will not grant him a new honour.'

I exchanged a solemn glance with father—and I admit we both burst into laughter.

Then I said, 'Surely, *you* can persuade "H.M." that it is now a little old-fashioned to deny a man his due because of this sort of indiscretion?'

'Well, unfortunately, he has broken the cardinal rule, "Thou shalt not be found out".'

There was no new honour for Sir John, and I was reminded of this incident when the Honours scandal burst.

Father had been somewhat indiscreet, too, it appeared—although this time not in the way to which 'H.M.' had taken exception in the Cowan affair. He had been shamelessly hawking 'honours' for political donations on a scale which made previous exponents of this practice seem like amateurs.

Like most people, I do not regard this cynical use of political influence with deep concern. Everyone knows that all parties in office have replenished their funds in this way. If father just happened to be rather more thorough, better organised and twice as imaginative as the others—well, that was Lloyd George. He had had a dual purpose in his distribution of honours: to make money and influence people. Well, the money would be for the Liberal Party—and for once they would be able to match the big Tory guns in the coming election. Good luck to father and the Liberal Party, I thought. Then there were the honours granted to men of influence—the Press tycoons and their editors. Another astute move by the Welsh Wizard.

The scandalised voices raised in Parliament caused me no anxiety. I was rather amused that father had gone one better than the Tories in the practice or malpractice which they had originated.

I had to admit, though, that he had been steering a little too close to the wind. There was the case of Sir Joseph Benjamin Robinson of South Africa.

Robinson was a highly successful 'property developer' who had bought some mining 'freeholds' for a song and then re-sold them to one of his own companies at an enormous profit. The action was condemned in the High Court some years later and Sir Joseph had to pay back no less than half a million pounds as compensation. The British Press roundly accused him of fraudulent conversion—and he took no action.

This was the man father had wanted to promote to the peerage.

When the truth leaked out, Sir Joseph wrote to father apparently more in sorrow than in anger, saying that he was surprised that the honour recommended to him had caused criticism, that he had never sought an elevation to the peerage and had reached an age when such matters no longer interested him.

A few days later, when a Coalition Liberal Party official called on Robinson to deliver the Prime Minister's answer to his letter, confirming that the recommendation of the peerage was now withdrawn, Sir Joseph interpreted it in his own way. He sighed deeply, drew out his cheque-book and said, "Well, how much more?——"

In July 1922 the Marquess of Salisbury, in the Lords, launched an attack. There were touts going about, it was reported, who claimed to have power of granting honours. Salisbury said that the principles that had been laid down for the bestowment of titles appeared to be as follows:

(*a*) For public services.
(*b*) For public services plus donations.
(*c*) For donations plus public services.
(*d*) For donations.

The Duke of Northumberland said, 'The Prime Minister's Party, insignificant in number and absolutely penniless four years ago, has in the course of those four years amassed an enormous Party chest, variously estimated at anything from a million to two million pounds . . . while groups of newspapers have been deprived of real independence by the sale of honours, and constitute a mere echo of Downing Street, from where they are controlled'.

Was it a coincidence, he demanded, that three persons connected with the principal newspapers in South Wales were honoured with titles? (Cardiff became known as the City of Dreadful Knights!)

He then quoted from letters, and said that a Minister of the Crown had offered a knighthood for £10,000, 'which need not be paid down all at once, but could be spread over a period of four years'. Honours on the never-never! This certainly was a new angle.

He quoted from another letter: 'I am authorised to offer you a knighthood or a baronetcy, not of the Order of the British Empire—no nonsense of that kind, but the real thing. A knighthood will cost you £12,000 and a baronetcy £35,000. You will be asked to meet someone in high authority, probably in Downing Street, and after the introduction but not until, say, three or four days before the List is announced you will be asked to pay £10,000 or £30,000 as the case may be—and I am permitted to take the balance, which represent the fees. There are only five knighthoods left on the June list——' warned this enterprising merchant.

These revelations caused so much protest from M.P.s that father proposed a Royal Commission to consider 'future procedure'.

'If it ever existed,' he said in the House, referring to this trade in honours, 'it was a discreditable system. It ought never to have existed. If it does exist, it ought to be terminated, and if there is any doubt on that point every step should be taken to deal with it.'

On the other hand, Asquith said that he did not think that contributions to Party funds should necessarily *disqualify* a citizen from receiving recognition for public services——

Which is where we came in.

The 'scandal' blew over. Temporarily.

The next chapter in the story concerns events which took place during the following election (1922).

Father and I were discussing the coming campaign and the prospects of victory. 'Anyway,' I said, 'one thing the Liberals can be certain of. With this mammoth Party fund you have accumulated, the Liberals will be able to contest every seat and put up the fight of all time.'

'Well—yes. I have put a hundred thousand at their disposal.'

'Only? But I heard there was close on a million available after the division with the Tory Party.'

'The Coalition Liberal Party Fund. That's me, you know. After all, Asquith and I have split up.'

I was rather puzzled. 'You mean, you control this fund personally?'

'Yes.'

'But on behalf of the Liberal Party?'

He said impatiently, 'What is the Liberal Party? Is it Asquith or is it me? I'm not handing the money over to those dunderheads.'

I was astonished. 'Let's get this clear. After the Coalition broke up, Bonar Law and you divided the two million between you. And what did Bonar do? Did he put it into a personal account to dispose of as he thought fit?'

I knew that Bonar Law had very properly handed his share of the 'donations' to the Conservative Party Secretary. I had believed father had observed the same propriety and placed the money in the hands of the Liberal Party.

He began to equivocate.

'I have no Party. I broke with Asquith—or he broke with me. It doesn't matter. Until I am satisfied that the Liberal Party is organised, unified in purpose, effectively managed, the money stays with me.'

I was alarmed, I told him that he was putting the cart before the horse, that the Liberal Party could have no unity of purpose or proper management unless the money squabble between its leaders was settled. How could there be a proper united front if the leaders did not trust each other?

Then I became suspicious. 'If you're not putting the money at the disposal of the Liberals—then what *are* you going to do with it?'

He made no answer.

I found out soon enough: he was buying newspaper properties. He was turning himself into a business tycoon like Northcliffe or Beaverbrook. In fact, with Beaverbrook's invaluable advice, he made some very shrewd purchases. But was this the reason he had given to the donors of these funds? And what if the newspaper ventures failed? How could he account for the money then?

Or *did* he have to account for it?

For some years there had been enquiries instigated by indignant Liberal officials, to determine precisely what right Lloyd George had in controlling this huge fund. They were subsequently told that its original political purpose was so wide, that no claim could be sustained in a court of law. A famous lawyer, Cyril Radcliffe, K.C., said that Lloyd George could with impunity gamble the money away on the Casino tables of Monte Carlo.

In the years that followed, as election followed election, he grudgingly parted with relatively small sums for political purposes, always complaining that larger sums would be wasted because the Liberal Party was neither efficiently managed nor staffed with worth-while candidates. The bitterness in the Party undermined its drive and purpose. Feuds raged; there were mass desertions to the Conservative and Labour ranks.

The cynical farce had become tragedy.

It was the end of the Liberal Party as a major force in politics. It was the end of Lloyd George as an effective political figure.

Why did he do it? Why, why, why? He did not need the vast sum. He was a successful and wealthy man. He earned about sixty thousand pounds from his Memoirs. He was probably the highest-paid journalist of his day—earning as much as thirty thousand pounds a year for a syndicated American column. Carnegie bestowed an annual income of ten thousand dollars on him.

Haig had been granted a hundred thousand pounds and an ancestral home for his war services. Father would have been ensured a quarter of a million on retirement from office had he only played the cards dealt him. But he had seen the chance of a 'coup'—a manœuvre of such subtlety and absolute finesse that he could not resist it. And he outsmarted himself.

> *This is the way the world ends,*
> *This is the way the world ends,*
> *This is the way the world ends,*
> *Not with a bang but a whimper.*

3

FATHER'S premiership ended in 1922, at the General Election in November, when he reaped the harvest of lack of vigilance, complacency on the one hand and over-astuteness on the other. He failed to adapt himself to the public trend leftwards—far too busy with international conferences, playing his rôle as Prime Minister of Europe—and so susceptible to feminine flattery and blandishments that he grew to believe himself infallible and invincible.

He tried to preserve the form of coalition government of the war years; but this was clearly an emergency compromise, and the Tories and the Labour members determined to strike out for independence. (In any case, they knew that in any coalition government Lloyd George would naturally assume leadership.)

The Liberal Party went divided to the polls—divided by the old feud of leadership between Asquith and Lloyd George, and suspicious over the machinations about the 'trust' fund which stayed in Lloyd George's private purse.

This combination of circumstances caused an unprecedented collapse of the Liberal Party in the election, and Labour became the official Opposition, with twenty-three seats more than the Asquithians (60) and the Lloyd Georgians (55) combined.

Father lost office as Prime Minister at the age of fifty-eight—at the height of his powers, in the fullness of experience, and with some twenty good years of vitality in his strong frame (he died in his eighty-third year). The political story of this period can be described in a single word: waste.

It was not that the task of forming a government no longer became possible. During the doldrum years, with Labour technically in and out of office, there were coalition governments in plenty—alliances with the Right, alliances with the middle, alliances by the Right with the Left and sometimes the middle;

a happy game of political musical chairs in which father in the old days would have nipped in double-quick and been first in the seat.

But the snap had gone out of his reactions. He let the Government of Bumblers, the Government of Snores and all the other tired cattle chew the cud. Bonar Law—able lieutenant, but never a true leader. Ramsay MacDonald with the lion-like head and the rabbit-like soul. Baldwin the Drifter—Chamberlain the Appeaser. What a crew! They distrusted Churchill, who had crossed the floor twice in his career. They distrusted and feared Lloyd George, who was too clever for his own good and would have walked all over them if given half a chance.

And the story of the times? National bankruptcy—mass unemployment—hunger marches—an arms race which became a contest between the rhinoceros and the tortoise, with Britain the tortoise—Jarrow—Mosley and the flash in the pan—destitution and corn being ploughed back into the land—malnutrition and fish being thrown back into the sea—an 'economy' in a state of chaos.

Father's personal life was in chaos, too.

Mother came home to Churt one day from Criccieth and found the main bedroom in confusion, with women's underclothes scattered all over the bed.

There was a final showdown with the old man—and mother left home for good. It was the end of a sick chapter more than thirty years long.

Father was engulfed by his hangers-on, flatterers, concubines.

I was summoned to Churt one day.

Father offered me a cigar. These visits of mine were very rare now—I had thought it fair to try to tranquillise mother, and spent far more time with her.

'Well, how are things with you, Dick?'

'Not bad.'

'Financially speaking?'

'Could be better.'

'Well, they're not building many bridges these days. How would you like to have a directorship on the board of a newspaper at two thousand pounds a year?'

'Who wouldn't?—But what do I know about newspapers?'

'Never mind. You'll learn.'

'Well, I'm certainly willing.'

'Good. This calls for a drink.'

It certainly did. Two thousand a year in those days was worth more than double its value today—and in times when there was general unemployment in the engineering industry it looked to me like a fortune!

The brandies were served and I sipped with deep satisfaction. Then I caught one of my father's characteristic side-glances—and I thought immediately that this was a 'move'.

Casually, I said, 'I suppose Gwilym will show me the ropes.' (Gwilym was closely associated with father in his business ventures.)

'Well, as a matter of fact, Gwilym is not on the board.'

'Not?'

He let the question hang for a moment and then said, 'I know you won't be difficult about this. But Gwilym refuses to sit on the board with Frances Stevenson'.

Frances Stevenson, the little schoolteacher, sitting on the board of a national newspaper! Gwilym wouldn't sit on the board with her, so father—possibly out of pique to annoy Gwilym, but probably out of fear of his girl friend and desire to placate her—decided to offer the seat to another member of the family. She would therefore no longer feel that she was an Outcast in Isolation.

I watched my father's eyebrows. He was brooding—watching me without appearing to notice my reaction at all—one of his tell-tale 'committee' looks; and suddenly I had an almost irresistible desire to laugh. The old man was back in the Cabinet, playing one Minister off against another—in difficulties about forming a government!

He said a little sheepishly, 'What are you grinning at?'

'Nothing. Nothing that would amuse you, sir. But I'm sorry I must decline the portfolio.'

I suppose that joke cost me two thousand a year—but I have never regretted it, really.

And how did father surmount his personal problem? I

wondered with considerable curiosity what he would do.

Well, he was equal to the emergency. A drastic remedy—but it worked. He sold his newspaper! Which proves that the old hand had really lost little of its cunning.

The legend of the Great Man remained, of course, and always will. He was an international figure. He no longer travelled; he 'visited' like royalty. When he went to America shortly after the dissolution of his government he got the sort of ticker-tape welcome accorded later to Lindbergh. He made up to fifteen speeches a day during his fabulous tour, and addressed the greatest open-air meeting of all time—an audience of four hundred thousand heard him through a relay of loudspeakers throughout the city.

My feelings vacillated. Sometimes I thought he was finally down for the count, and then I was quickened to fresh hope by some remarkable show of vigour. When he returned from the States I saw him several times, always hoping that he would show the old enthusiasm for making another fight. Yet I was always disappointed. He needed my mother's sympathetic, staunch heart to rally his will.

Things were far too comfortable for him. He had a vast income from his literary earnings, the enormous 'trust' fund to indulge his fancy for financial speculation, and an immense property in Surrey, Churt, with its ever-increasing acreage. He was content to vegetate in luxury, surrounded by bevies of female retainers.

Many of them had an official position. There were bee-keepers, land-girls, lady filing-clerks, librarians, maids of all sorts—or just plain 'visitors', gallant and giggling ladies with exotic airs and graces.

There was a Mrs H., a grass widow, with immense 'magnetism', an earlier edition of Marilyn Monroe who left me a little breathless when I first met her. I asked father what her 'official' function was, as she had greeted my innocent enquiry with uninhibited peals of merriment.

'Just a friend,' father said, rather peevishly. Then, with an effort to convince: 'I feel sorry for the girl. Her husband has run off with Another Woman.'

It seemed to me that sympathies were unnecessary, as Mrs H.

was in top form, as happy as a nightingale, with a thrilling tone of voice.

There was a French girl who 'translated'. It seemed an unnecessary refinement to have a resident translator, whether into or from the French, but doubtless it added varied colour to the scene.

I got into lukewarm water one day when the telephone rang and I answered the enquiry to speak to the mistress of the house with the words—quite involuntarily uttered—'Which one?'

One day, visiting father, I found the windows screened with bars. Naturally, I asked why he was taking this precaution, and he told me that there had been an outbreak of burglaries in the neighbourhood. It was not a very convincing explanation—but not too bad an effort made, as it was, impromptu.

My question was answered when Frances Stevenson, who had been absent on the Continent, returned with what I have been told was an 'adopted' daughter.

Then there was an American lady, an actress all the way from Hollywood, who spent some time with father. She was a real queen of the silver screen, though not quite as young as she appeared at first glance. I remember her chiefly because she made telephone calls—without anyone's knowledge—to her friends in the States. Homesick, no doubt. Father did not know about it till the quarterly account arrived from the telephone company. It appeared that she had had daily chats just to say 'hello' to New York and Hollywood.

Well, no doubt a host should not quibble about such items of expenditure to entertain his guests.

The ladies came and went—and I have not the least doubt that some of them really exercised a perfectly proper occupation. But one day, after a rather mellowing dinner, as I was leaving amidst a girlish chorus of farewells and looked a little hazily at the confusing array of variedly pretty faces, I remarked (in the immortal words of Dorothy Parker), 'Yes—if all you ladies were laid end to end, I wouldn't be the least surprised.'

4

FATHER'S ménage was so unusual by standards of Western civilisation that I was sometimes impelled by a very natural curiosity to make my own investigations as to how it was run, what the 'drill' was, whether there were any sort of Rules of Conduct. (I believe that eastern harems were really places of quite rigorous discipline—for the female inmates, that is.) For instance, how were the natural passions of feminine jealousy kept under control amongst so much complexity of personal relationship? And I could not but remark the relative youthfulness of the women—their lord was about thirty to forty years older than most of them; so that the further question naturally arose in my mind—What was the appeal to the ladies, apart from the rather obvious one that he was a very wealthy man? He could not regularise his relationships with them nor give their children his name.

I found myself in confidential discussion about father with a rather soft, dark young woman.

She giggled. 'He's a funny gentleman, isn't he?'

'He amuses you, does he?'

'Could say.'

'Tell me something he said that amused you.'

'Oh, Major Richard!'

'Go on. Tell me.'

'Well, let's see. . . . There's a story about a preacher . . . and in the end he says to the congregation, "My brethren, where would you rather be—with the five wise virgins in the light—or with the five foolish virgins in the dark?" '

This was the style of conversation I had with several of the migrant staff. From one of them I tried to elicit if there was any point of common interest between father and herself. Was she interested in literature? In music? In politics? In travel? In farming?—There was a shake of the head and a giggle to each question.

'But you say you do like him?'

'Oh, I do. . . . Oh, Major Richard, your father is so *strong* . . .!'

Jealousy, I found, did not seem to enter into the picture at all. Quite the reverse. The amiability was so extensive and all-embracing that one of the principals of the establishment—a foundation member, in fact—introduced her sister into the household. Whether or not the original intention had been a social one I cannot say; but the outcome was that she, too, became integrated into this unorthodox family.

The old man's general attitude to this preponderant feminine influence was a mixture of the patriarchal and the mystical. Sometimes he would condescend to jollification and benevolence. At other times, he was sunk in depression, gloom and despondency, so that the favoured ones in vain tried to charm him into a good mood.

I think he must have seen the futility of this empty, endless pursuit of the sensual. I had never before known him to be so profoundly harassed, so constantly, morbidly preoccupied with himself, so frequently querulous and self-pitying. There were times when ennui seemed to be insupportable, and I grew to feel anxious about his depressions.

We were at supper one evening with some of his 'family', and he was so listless and indifferent to all and everything about him that even his table manners began to offend. He leaned one elbow by his plate and shovelled soup rather haphazardly into his mouth so that some of it clung to his moustache. He ignored all efforts to coax him into conversation; and I could feel him working up to an accumulated mood of grievance and self-pity.

Nobody loved him. The people had rejected him. His friends had deserted him. His wife had left him. His eldest daughter would not speak to him. His eldest son disapproved of him.

I felt a tightening in my stomach at the thought that he was about to mingle silent tears with his soup.

I pretended to try to tell one of his favourite stories. '. . . Now how does it go?—There was a publican in Wales, who was offered a horse by a traveller for a night's lodgings—Or was it a dog?—Anyway, the man said this is a remarkable horse or dog because it can recite the Welsh alphabet—or was it something else? . . .'

Father turned to me impatiently, wiping his moustache. 'Now, for heaven's sake, Dick,' he said in Welsh, 'dry up.' He ruminated a moment or two, then put down his napkin.

'As a matter of fact, this isn't a bad story—if told properly.'

He told it briefly, perfectly, timing it exactly to the taste of his particular audience. The laugh was automatic, uninhibited.

He pushed away his plate, sat up and began again.

In a few minutes he was well away, his audience were in fits and the table was humming. Later in the course of the evening he caught my eye and realised that I had deliberately set him off—tried to recapture the old Merlin that was still there, locked up inside him.

When I left that night, he saw me off, walking with me a little way, his mood somewhat mellowed.

'I suppose you did that deliberately, Dick. You could have told that story of yours well enough.'

'Well—my name's Lloyd George, too, isn't it?'

'What are you trying to prove—that I can still be the life and soul of the Party?' I made no answer, and he said, 'Why should I? Haven't I had enough? Don't you think I've done enough? Have I no right to peace and rest now? Let them carry on in office. Who wants it? Why should I carry the burden till my back breaks? Is that what you want?' He went on in this strain until I felt almost unnerved. Who wanted office and responsibility except an idiot—when he could have peace? He had had all of it in his time and he assured me that only the insatiable, the stupid—those obsessed with power—carried on till they were emptied like husks.

I said to him, 'It's because power no longer has any attraction for you that you should go back. That's when you're really fit for office. There are three million unemployed in this country.'

He was silent for a long time. Neither of us spoke till we said farewell. Then he touched me rather in the old way, suddenly, and said, 'Come back soon, Dick. Don't leave it so long till the next time.'

The old boy is really utterly lonely, I thought—and then the acid undertone: I wonder whose turn it is when the lights are out?

From the house, there suddenly came the sound of a gramophone playing ragtime. Father made an angry gesture. The mice knew he hated jazz, and seized their chance the moment he stepped out of the front door.

5

THE reader will probably find a comic note in this account of father's modern seraglio; and if it did not concern a great man at the peak of his powers—and a time when there was a crying need for his serivces—it could hardly be more than amusing. I am not much of a moralist, and I do not care to add my voice to any chorus of condemnation. But I was concerned at the time at the dreadful waste of his talents, at the ominous softening of his will to political action, at the diminution of his stature in public life. Faster and faster went the descent. In 1922, beaten once. In 1924 again. And then progressively, with all his mental sinews slackening, he was letting go—letting the course of events dictate completely.

The descent was uncanny, almost unprecedented, as remarkable as his early rise. All my very worst fears—and worse. Everything was beginning to go. This formidable man, this super being, was becoming an absurdity—*pathetic* to those who knew him in public life.

How could they take him seriously now? How could he even begin to rally a Party?

What had become of all his friends? Where was the sound of the high and the mighty in his drawing-room? In the old days, the companies which filled our house could have posed tableaux for historic tapestries. The Elders had gone for ever; the New Men ignored him; the Young knew nothing of him and wanted to know nothing.

Distinguished visitors from abroad occasionally went to see him—as though they were visiting a famous landmark or historic monument.

He produced pamphlets. He solved the problems of unemployment, transport, coal and power, agriculture, industry—on paper. His technique was to appoint experts to study these questions—

at the cost of the Liberal Political Fund, renamed the Lloyd George Trust Fund—which he would then study at second hand. They were arid compositions, now long forgotten. Lloyd George never was a pamphleteer. It was always the personal touch, the oratorical flame, which ignited the response in his vast audiences.

When there was the chance of alliances with Tories he objected because he would not see Labour's reform policy annihilated. When there was a chance of an alliance with Labour, he objected because he refused to be a 'ladder supporting the incompetent scaffolders'.

He was rationalising, inventing excuses to himself as well as to others for inactivity, for the life of ease and sybaritic pleasure, luxury travel.

He was getting to be capricious beyond bounds. On board a yacht, he once instructed his secretary to signal an Italian cruiser to relay a message to land, cancelling an appointment for lunch! (Or perhaps he was re-living the days of his ministerial glory.) These prima-donna traits now made him intolerant of any sort of criticism, and he deliberately surrounded himself with those who were content to nod their heads with the predictable regularity of rocking-horses.

He began to lose his common touch, his sense of the atmosphere, of the 'need' of his audience.

He got the shock of his life in the House of Commons when he obstructed a Labour measure to reduce the working hours of miners (which would have the effect slightly of increasing the rate of wages), regulate production quotas and put a levy on home sold coal. (It was a muddled Bill, but should have been handled sympathetically by L. G. because its *intentions* were absolutely sound and in line with his own policy.)

He attacked the Bill in a sledge-hammer mood—because it was Labour's Bill, and not his. And when he was done, a young Welsh M.P., Aneurin Bevan, rose and pointed his finger at the Father of the House. 'The veins of the miners are already shrunken white,' he stormed. 'Better to have dearer coal than cheaper colliers—— We are asking you, for once, to be decent to the miners —not to use all your parliamentary skill, all your rhetoric, in an act of pure demagogy to expose the mining community to more misery.'

The great Radical sat silent under the tongue-lashing of the youngster—that voice of his own youth echoing back to him. Thus had the young Lloyd George, in the days when he was championing the weak and impoverished, wielded the axe against the petrified giants of the Tory forest.

His judgment was becoming impaired. There was his extraordinary flirtation with Hitler. He visited the dictator at Berchtesgaden during a trip to Germany, and came back with deep admiration for the 'personality' of the 'great leader'. Hitler had stuffed his head with a lot of lying nonsense about his pacific intentions; and father was overwhelmed by the clockwork precision with which industry was run. He tried to convince me that we had misjudged the Fuehrer, who wanted nothing except to make Germany prosperous and the world safe from Bolshevism.

I told him that I had it on the highest authority that Hitler was going to invade Poland in 1939, France 1940, Russia 1941 and us in 1946 (if he could).

'Who told you that?' he snorted.

'I read it in Hitler's book, Mein Kampf. You ought to buy a copy. It only costs seven and six. It would have saved you the expense of a trip to Germany.'

Father looked at me suspiciously. 'If he said that, it was only for German consumption. Besides,' he added, rallying, 'nobody who really meant it would have told you.'

'Ah,' I pointed out, 'that's what he wants you to think.'

In spite of everything, there were flashes which showed that the power was still there.

The appeasement which led to the invasion of Abyssinia by Mussolini, and the defection over sanctions that followed it, brought forth a fighting speech in the manner of the old days— described by Churchill as one of the greatest parliamentary performances of all time, which was a handsome tribute from an old friend, and as 'that extraordinarily brilliant speech, which has shown me that the Rt. Hon. Gentleman has not lost the least atom of vigour which I remember in this House nearly thirty years ago', which was handsomer—coming from the one who was the target of it, Prime Minister Stanley Baldwin.

Father concluded with these words: 'The choice before us is whether we shall make a last effort at Geneva for peace and security, or whether by a cowardly surrender we shall break all the promises we have made and hold ourselves up to the shame of our children and their children's children.' Then, with his old dramatic gesture, pointing at the apprehensive figures of Baldwin and his Front Bench colleagues, 'Tonight we have had a cowardly surrender, and *there* are the cowards.'

But it seems a pity that this call for courageous action was not heard by the one who made it. Time was long overdue for him to return to the arena—as a contestant, not as a spectator in the critics' box.

6

THERE was the tragi-comedy of his seraglio—and there
was a more serious and dramatic business.

I was visiting Churt one day and I found father with
Viscount Snowden and his wife. These friends lived near by, and
were frequent visitors, but I had never noticed before the curi-
ously contradictory manner of the gracious lady, who was sometimes friendly and sometimes distinctly edgy in her attitude to
father. Father's manner with a handsome woman was always all
of a piece—he was out to make an impression; and Lady S. certainly was a fine-looking creature, tall, with a superb figure, full
of vitality. She was a woman of wit and intelligence.

She sometimes played the piano, conscious of the delightful
composition of light and design she made, I think, as she sat there,
now and then turning to face her audience or duettist—father
often sang with her—and improvising in a humorous and quite
accomplished manner.

Father's tenor tones blended with the melody, and watching
them together I noticed, with considerable uneasiness, certain
characteristic glances—the whimsically raised eyebrows, the
somewhat carnivorous smile, the lady's warning look and lowered
gaze; and I feared that it might be more than the music that would
soon be blending.

Now the reader may wonder a little—as I write of this period
(I think it was the early 'thirties)—that father must have been
close to seventy at the time, and surely his days of Edwardian
gallantry were at an end.

Well, it was not so. He had quite a remarkable physique still,
and he had fined down a little from his early sixties. He wore his
clothes in a way I have never seen matched—always very dapper.
There was, however, no foppishness or stiffness about him, but a
careless perfection of style. He was weather-beaten from his

farming life and travels, and the tan set off a silvery mane strikingly and quite beautifully. He had a chevalier-like distinction; and the weather-beaten features contrasting with the ethereal head gave extra facets to his personality. With an attractive woman he was as much to be trusted as a Bengal tiger with a gazelle.

I became conscious of deep gloom, and then, as I continued to observe, alarm.

What about Lord Snowden, one might ask? Apart from being something of an absent-minded intellectual, I think he would have been profoundly shocked if he knew father's habits and predilections. I think he saw just as much as I did—an attractive, gallant elderly gentleman, working very hard to charm a warm, vital and handsome woman. Harmless, one might suppose, unless you knew who you were dealing with. Lloyd George, unhappily, was never a respecter of his friends' wives.

Snowden was an attractive man, with a lean and haggard charm; but he was not a well man. He was a cripple, as I remember, and possibly, an invalid. His wife seemed to be twice his size, a 'statuesque' creature and with a gloss of fine health and energy, a perfect partner for the experienced and still athletic Lothario who was paying court to her under her husband's nose.

I left them that night with a deep uneasiness which haunted me for a time—and then, in the natural course of events and with other things to think about, I dismissed the matter from my mind.

One afternoon, I was at Churt running over some of the farm management details, when a problem cropped up which I wanted to talk over with father. I looked for him—and found him deep in conversation with Lady Snowden. Lord Snowden was nowhere to be seen.

I had not expected her visit, and thought of retreating, when suddenly she became aware of my presence. Instead of greeting me, she suddenly broke off her serious conversation and went out into the garden very abruptly, leaving father alone with me. It was the act of an emotionally strained woman who could not trust herself to behave with conventional decorum.

I hesitated. 'Sorry if I intruded, but something cropped up——'

'Intruded? Intruded? What do you mean by that?' he snapped. 'What do you want, Dick?'

'I obviously have intruded,' I said, incensed. 'All right, it doesn't matter. What I wanted to see you about can wait. Don't leave your guest on her own.'

I walked out, annoyed with the old man and thoroughly depressed.

I tried to forget about it, to brush it aside as something that could not possibly concern me any longer. The child cry, *Don't hurt mamie!* had never completely ceased echoing in my heart, even though now she was beyond hurt; but I knew in a rational sense that this part of it was all over and done with.

None of your business, Richard Lloyd George. Forget it.

These were the sort of things I told myself at the end of the day; and I thought that by evening I had cleared it completely from my mind and emotions.

In the evening, during dinner, father ignored the little interruption of his *tête-à-tête* with Lady Snowden, and I carefully avoided referring to it.

After dinner, we went for a walk on the estate, wandering into the orchards and discussing the year's crops. Father was in a fairly jovial mood—he had been cordial during dinner—and chatted in a friendly way on our pleasant evening stroll. He tapped the fruit with his stick, then picked it and rubbed the bloom.

He was in a mood to philosophise. Nature, he said, replenished itself—well, naturally. A man, a tree, a plant; they were all one. He was becoming expansive, all embracing in his analogies. Life —the sap rising in the trees—and all the bounty of the earth—they obeyed no conventions or rules of conduct except to grow, to flower, to reproduce their kind. What had our trifling little codes to do with the work of procreation? He waved his stick, he gestured. I was an audience of thousands he was addressing from Tower Hill, from the plinth in Trafalgar Square. He was working hard, building up to his climaxes artistically. Obviously, he had been thinking what he wanted to say with special care. I should have felt flattered, the target of such artistry normally reserved for thousands.

Unfortunately, I was just plain, dull Dick, his son, who just could not seem to understand what he was talking about. He became a little impatient, then a trifle irascible. He repeated some of the analogies more emphatically. Still I remained obtuse.

'Well—say something, Dick. Tell me what *you* think? Don't you realise the point I'm making—nature must run its course like a wild, all-embracing vine, constantly turning to the sun, irresistibly scaling the highest orchard wall—upwards, upwards!'

I heard myself say, 'Do you think it right to make love to the wife of a cripple?'

For a second I thought I was in danger of being lashed by his stick. He moved towards me, his hand raised, and although I am tall and fit—taller than he—I had a momentary sensation of fright.

Then he pulled himself together; and I heard our deep breathing in the stillness of night in that orchard.

The strange anger between father and son, which always seems to wrestle with the love between them, gave way in my heart to compassion; but we did not reach out to each other, either by touch or word. I had always felt him as big in size, but now he seemed small, no taller than his inches; and frail, too, somehow. I tried to reach out to him—but he moved away and we were alone.

We returned to the house our separate ways.

7

WHEN thinking of my father, I sometimes recall an incident which, though seemingly trivial, must be significant to me. I was trying to coax some life into a stubborn coal-fire one morning. In my engineering pride, I fancied myself quite an expert hand in lighting a fire, but in this case the coal had been damp, the wood splinters too sparse and I had been on my knees on and off for almost an hour trying to woo some response from the large precarious edifice.

My father came into the room, rubbing his hands and complaining about the cold. He looked at my smoking structure, all promise and no fulfilment, and impatiently planted his boot right in the centre of it. Immediately, like a faithful hound answering the call of a tyrannical master, the thing came to life. Flames shot up; in a moment the large grate was blazing like a furnace.

I turned and looked, speechless, at father, grinning in triumph down at me on my knees. 'There you are, Dick. Easy!'

I said to him, 'I now know the secret of your success. It's plain, twenty-two carat, diamond-monogrammed, unadulterated luck.'

He roared.

For those of my readers as yet unborn I would urge that in deciding a choice of parents they should carefully avoid having a genius in the family.

Can you imagine how it must be—say, in the case of a young would-be mountaineer born to someone like Sir Edmund Hillary? He spreads out the map of the world, and father says, 'There you are—Everest. That's the highest mountain in the world. I scaled it. These—the Caucasian Heights. They're not quite as high. I used them for practice. This is an interesting one—K2. It's the most difficult of all mountains, if not the highest. The view from the summit is rather rewarding, though—I'll show you my snaps. If I were you, I'd try a new planet, son.'

I recall an incident which sometimes comes back to me in my dreams. I was an apprentice engineer at the time, just starting my career. Working on a construction job at Tilbury, I would wear the roughest of clothes which frequently became stained with slime or grease. Crossing Parliament Square from the Westminster Station of the underground one evening, I was too tired after a hard day's work to note the surprising absence of traffic; and it was not until I had reached Downing Street that I saw a line of police constables filling the roadway ahead.

When I tried to break through between two policemen, they stopped me. 'Where do you think you're going, mate?'

'Home,' I said.

'And where's that?'

'I'm Richard Lloyd George. I live at No. 11.'

'And I'm Mary Pickford,' the bobby said jovially. 'Go on—'op it.'

I protested. I was dying to get home and have a hot bath. The massive line of policemen would not budge. I went down the line, desperately trying to establish my identity—but it was no use. After a while, the laughter and ribald remarks ceased to be funny. I was feeling a little groggy with exhaustion, but no one cared. It was rather like a bad dream. You begin to wonder. Has everyone suddenly gone mad? Or is it you who has been living in a world of illusion all this time? Are you really the son of the Chancellor of the Exchequer? You may well understand why I have sometimes dreamed of this incident, and why, after some fifty years I still remember it so vividly.

It was always difficult to live permanently in the shadow of father's greatness.

'Is your name really Lloyd George?' (How many times have I heard this question on my travels thousands of miles from home.)

'Yes. Richard Lloyd George.'

'Are you related to David Lloyd George?' (Yes, oh yes, oh yes, indeed, really and truly, yes and yes.)

'No. He's related to me,' I would sometimes answer with mock good-humour.

It was never much use even trying to compete—on any level, or achieve true independence.

I remember when father became Prime Minister. I was at home on leave then, too, and shared in the great sense of family pride and excitement. But that was not all I felt. All the conflicting emotions I ever felt towards the man who had so often hurt us—mother and me—swept through my consciousness. I thought, 'If they had known what I knew about him, he would never have even become the humblest member of the House of Commons!'

And when he came home in triumph from Versailles—the Man Who Won the War—the King of England rode to Victoria Station to meet him amidst the multitudes—the King to pay him tribute, too—and I knew that my father's place in history was for ever assured as one of our country's great leaders, I looked at myself in the mirror. I did not seem any different—I saw no change in myself . . . and I wondered what the others felt at that moment —Gwilym, Megan, all of us, who had lived in his shadow. All his life he had drawn on the energies and fed on the love of those about him, like a monster greedy child who demands everything as his right and gives nothing of himself in return. He had used people like isotopes, charging himself with their energies; but there would be nothing for us but the reflected glow of his greatness.

Megan never had the chance to live her own life fully; neither had any of us. Always he had need of support. My mother protected him for thirty years. My youngest sister was to become his shadow. But in his later life, he turned to others; and in the end we were almost strangers, a family broken and divided when my mother's gentleness and endurance had passed their breaking point. His eldest son and his eldest daughter he disinherited.

What true friendship had he ever formed, which remained to him in his long years of decline? Had he ever been anything but the spoiled child whom everyone had to protect and whom he rewarded with ingratitude? He had hangers-on by the score, and concubines, procurers and flatterers.

That was my father. He was a man it was impossible not to admire, almost impossible not to love, barely possible not to forgive, with qualities and gifts that would have graced a dozen men; but the selfishness and egotism which fed on every form of earthly success and flattery in the end diminished him until he was small indeed.

8

RIGHT through the pre-war period and up to 1939, Lloyd George remained potentially the greatest statesman in Parliament—always without office. His attacks on the tragic errors of government and foreign policy read like wisdom after the events. On Chamberlain's policy of appeasement he might have expressed opinions voiced six years later. He castigated Chamberlain over Munich—protesting that the constant snubs to Russia would alienate that vast military nation. It had, as we know, precisely that effect; and had Lloyd George's pre-war policy of an alliance with Russia and Czechoslovakia been effected, it is possible that even Hitler, with all his aggressiveness, would have feared to launch his armies against two fronts simultaneously—the fear of this was a permanent hindrance to the Nazi military programme which Mr Chamberlain accommodatingly removed. Lloyd George went about singing Russia's virtues as an ally as though she had already achieved the age of sputniks.

'Chamberlain is a self-mesmerised rabbit who has persuaded himself, because he disapproves of her, that Russia does not exist. His foreign policy operates in a vacuum!' he said to me, despairingly.

He brought Chamberlain down with all his old fighting fervour in a single glorious speech, which closed with the death-knell words: 'The Prime Minister has appealed for sacrifice. The nation is prepared for every sacrifice so long as it has leadership. I say solemnly that the Prime Minister should give an example of sacrifice, because there is nothing he can contribute more to victory than that he should sacrifice the seals of office.'

Chamberlain fell; and Churchill formed a government.

His old friend sought the old man to lend his voice in the highest council chamber, in the War Cabinet.

'No, no. My doctor says I can no longer command the grasp of detail necessary to run a government department.'

That difficulty can be removed, urged Winston. Lloyd George need only attend War Cabinet meetings. He need not be responsible for any ministerial department.

'No—Chamberlain and I will never agree. Whilst he opposes my appointment my presence will only cause friction.'

'But Chamberlain now declares that he has no opposition to your appointment. There will be no difficulty. The greatest force in the First World War's council chamber will be an inspiration to the leadership of the Second. The country remembers. The country's spirit will be strengthened by your presence in the War Cabinet.'

Churchill sent for a mutual friend, Beaverbrook, to try to persuade Lloyd George to accept. For three hours the old comrades talked and talked; and then Beaverbrook triumphantly telephoned to Churchill that the old man was willing to return!

But no. At the last moment Lloyd George changed his mind.

There were no official excuses this time; just a general complaint repeated constantly in private, 'I am not going in with that gang!'

A 'gang' led by Churchill? A 'gang' with a will to fight at last? A 'gang' with all its personal jealousies and ambitions subordinated, who now recalled the legend of The Man Who Won the War and looked on Lloyd George as an idol, and would have listened to him as an oracle?

Why did he not join the War Cabinet?

Was it a 'move'?

Yes, there were some private advisers—fools and worse—who whispered because they dared not raise their voices: 'Let them fail. Let the government collapse. Then you shall Take Over.'

Let them fail; let the country bleed so that you should Take Over. Which was the *gang*'?

But I don't think that Lloyd George really listened to these vampires. I think it was just another excuse.

The truth was he had lost his nerve. The old war-horse had lorded it in the peaceful pasture so long that the weight of armour frightened him.

He pottered about on his farm; he read old Memoirs about the days of his glory; and he complained interminably about the war, the leaders, the policy.

After my mother died, he married Frances Stevenson.

No one came to the wedding. The family refused to attend. Even Megan, loyal, loving, devoted, dominated all her life by him, bitterly cried, 'I shall never forgive him!'

In the end, she did. When he was on his death-bed, she held his hand—and Frances Stevenson held the other.

But let not this be the end.

When Winston Churchill made his after-Dunkirk speech in which he promised us nothing but blood, toil, tears, and sweat—and brought us peace, victory, security—father went to congratulate him, grasping his hand with tears in his eyes. Then he turned and they went their separate ways. It was the last time they met—the one who had first lit the torch, and the other who grasped it from his weakening grip.

Let us close the book on that handclasp.

INDEX